The Story of Jack and the Beanstalk

A Pantomime

Ronald Parr

A Samuel French Acting Edition

SAMUELFRENCH-LONDON.CO.UK
SAMUELFRENCH.COM

Copyright © 1954 by Ronald Parr
All Rights Reserved

THE STORY OF JACK AND THE BEANSTALK is fully protected under the copyright laws of the British Commonwealth, including Canada, the United States of America, and all other countries of the Copyright Union. All rights, including professional and amateur stage productions, recitation, lecturing, public reading, motion picture, radio broadcasting, television and the rights of translation into foreign languages are strictly reserved.

ISBN 978-0-573-06431-9

www.samuelfrench-london.co.uk

www.samuelfrench.com

For Amateur Production Enquiries

United Kingdom and World excluding North America

plays@SamuelFrench-London.co.uk

020 7255 4302/01

Each title is subject to availability from Samuel French, depending upon country of performance.

CAUTION: Professional and amateur producers are hereby warned that *THE STORY OF JACK AND THE BEANSTALK* is subject to a licensing fee. Publication of this play does not imply availability for performance. Both amateurs and professionals considering a production are strongly advised to apply to the appropriate agent before starting rehearsals, advertising, or booking a theatre. A licensing fee must be paid whether the title is presented for charity or gain and whether or not admission is charged.

The professional rights in this play are controlled by Samuel French Ltd, 52 Fitzroy Street, London, W1T 5JR.

No one shall make any changes in this title for the purpose of production. No part of this book may be reproduced, stored in a retrieval system, or transmitted in any form, by any means, now known or yet to be invented, including mechanical, electronic, photocopying, recording, videotaping, or otherwise, without the prior written permission of the publisher. No one shall upload this title, or part of this title, to any social media websites.

The right of Ronald Parr to be identified as author of this work has been asserted by him in accordance with Section 77 of the Copyright, Designs and Patents Act 1988

AUTHOR'S NOTE

The Story of Jack and the Beanstalk was first presented at Nottingham Playhouse on 23rd December 1953. Production was by John Harrison and Jack was played by Daphne Slater.

Stage directions, here given from the actors' viewpoint, may freely be adapted to a simple or elaborate production. At Nottingham Playhouse, Jack and Alice climbed a rope-ladder Beanstalk, but it is not essential that they should be seen doing this.

As the Beanstalk Fairy points out, Mangel-Wurzel-on-the-Wold lies "on the fringe of Fairyland". Though its inhabitants do not suspect this, they are naturally affected by a climate in which the familiar and the fantastic flourish side by side. Of the incongruities thus produced, they remain quite unconscious.

R. P.

CHARACTERS

Mrs Durden, landlady of *The Flying Horse*
Jack, her son
Alderman Grimshank, the Mayor
Alice, his daughter
Gaffer Dribbledrip
Simple Simon
The Beanstalk Fairy
Maisie, a cow
1st Child
2nd Child
Croaker, a semi-fairy butler
Mrs Croaker
1st Fairy
2nd Fairy
Sir Mortimer Mortiboy
Mr Blenkinsop, from the BBC
Village Children and Fairies

SYNOPSIS OF SCENES

ACT I   The Village Green of Mangel-Wurzel-on-the-Wold
ACT II Inside the Giant's Castle
ACT III The Village Green again—with a difference

MUSICAL NUMBERS

All the music needed for use in this Pantomime is now out of copyright in its original form, the various composers having been dead for more than fifty years. The composers' original work may therefore be used without permission or payment. But, in the case of some items, there may be new arrangements that are subject to copyright, and if any of these copyright arrangements are used, permission must be sought in the usual way from the publishers of the music or from the Performing Rights Society. Permission to perform the Pantomime does not include permission to use copyright arrangements of the music.

ACT I

1	Chorus Tune: *Girls and Boys come out to Play* (Traditional)	CHILDREN
2	Song Tune: *There was a Little Man* (Traditional)	JACK and CHORUS
3	Mangel-Wurzel	MRS DURDEN, GRIMSHANK, GAFFER and SIMON
4a	Chorus Tune: *Baa baa, Black Sheep* (Traditional)	CHILDREN
4b	Chorus *Repeat of No. 1*	CHILDREN
5a	Chorus Tune: *Good Night, Ladies* (Traditional)	CHILDREN
5b	Ensemble Tune: *Who Killed Cock Robin?* (Traditional)	JACK, GRIMSHANK, MRS DURDEN, GAFFER and CHILDREN
6a	Prelude, Flower Song (*Carmen*—Bizet)	INSTRUMENTAL
6b	Chorus Tune: *Toreador's Song* (*Carmen*—Bizet)	JACK, ALICE, GAFFER, SIMON and CHILDREN
6c	Tango Any tango music may be used	INSTRUMENTAL
7	Duet Tune: *If You Go In* (*Iolanthe*—Sullivan)	JACK and BEANSTALK FAIRY

Musical settings are available for Nos. 3, 10 and 14 on application.

ACT II

8	Duet Tune: *I Once was a Very Abandoned Person* (*Ruddigore*—Sullivan)	CROAKER and MRS CROAKER
9a	Chorus Tune: *How Beautifully Blue the Sky* (*Pirates of Penzance*—Sullivan)	FAIRIES
9b	Chorus Tune: *Soldiers' Chorus* (*Faust*—Gounod)	FAIRIES
10	*Never Trust the Natives*	SIR MORTIMER, JACK and ALICE
10a	Chorus *Repeat of No. 5a*	SIR MORTIMER, JACK and ALICE

ACT III

11	Ballad Tune: *When Maiden Loves* (*Yeoman of the Guard*—Sullivan)	JACK
12	Chorus Tune: *Come Lasses and Lads* (Traditional)	CHILDREN
13	Song Tune: *When I was a Lad* (*H.M.S. Pinafore*—Sullivan)	BLENKINSOP and CHORUS
14	*What's the Use of a Golden Egg?*	MRS DURDEN
15	Trio Tune: *The Painful Plough* (Traditional) (This is the signature tune to the BBC feature, *Country Magazine*)	GRIMSHANK, GAFFER and SIMON
15a	Chorus *Repeat of No. 12*	CHILDREN
16	Finale *Reprises of Nos. 15, 5a, 7, 10, 14, 3 and verse to Bridal Chorus* (*Lohengrin*—Wagner)	FULL COMPANY

THE STORY OF JACK AND THE BEANSTALK*

ACT I

Scene—*The Village Green of Mangel-Wurzel-on-the-Wold.*

The shops and houses are crazy Cotswold or tumbledown Tudor L *is "The Flying Horse" Inn with a picture signboard;* R *is a shop with the sign "Family Grimshank Butcher". There are practical doors and windows to both. The place has a delapidated air—missing tiles and thatch, etc. There are several "To Let" and "For Sale" notices. Up* C *is a well, from which the Beanstalk later ascends. There is a bench* L.

When the Curtain *rises,* Gaffer Dribbledrip *is dozing on the bench.* Simple Simon *is sweeping in front of the butcher's shop. The* Village Children *enter singing. They dance round Simon, pulling him along with them.*

No. 1 CHORUS (Children)

Children. Girls and boys come out to play;
While the school-bell rings away
We'll pretend we do not hear
So gather round and never fear
Father's frown or teacher's cane:
We will never go back again;
Here we'll stay in the village street
Demanding our Coronation treat.

Simon. Now stop it I tell you!
Now drop it I tell you!
You'll cop it I tell you!
Let go!

Children.   Silly fool!
Simple Simon's a fool!

Simon. Run away!
Go and play
Or pop off to school!
You've lessons to learn,
I've wages to earn!

Children. We've just come to do you a jolly good turn! (*They spin him round*)

---

*N.B. Paragraph 3 on page ii of this Acting Edition regarding photocopying and video-recording should be carefully read.

SIMON. I tell you I'm busy!
You're making me dizzy!
CHILDREN. Pretend you're Dick Whittington turning again!
Yes, turn him again!
SIMON. Just you wait!
I'll complain
To your pas and your mas and they'll give you the cane!
CHILDREN. Spin him round, spin him round
Till he sinks to the ground!

(ALICE *enters from the shop*)

ALICE. Children! Stop!

(*They release* SIMON. *He reels about giddily*)

1ST CHILD. Why, it's Alice!
CHILDREN. Good morning, Alice.
ALICE. It doesn't seem a very good morning for poor Simple Simon. What *have* you been doing? And why aren't you in school?
1ST CHILD. Shall we tell her?
CHILDREN. No!
ALICE. But why not?
1ST CHILD (*importantly*) Because our business is with your father...
SIMON. My gaffer.
2ND CHILD. His Washup the Mayor.

(*Boos*)

1ST CHILD. And prominent spoilsport.

(*Groans*)

ALICE. Oh dear! I'm afraid father isn't in a very good mood.
1ST CHILD. Wait till he hears what *we've* got to say.
ALICE. But why not tell me first? Perhaps I could help.

(JACK *enters from* "*The Flying Horse*")

1ST CHILD. Then you'd better ask our leader and spokesman, Jack Durden.
ALICE. Jack? Why, Jack would do anything for me.
JACK. Of course I would, Alice. Anything in the world!

(*They embrace*)

1ST CHILD. Three cheers for Jack and Alice. Hip, hip...

(*The* CHILDREN *give three cheers.*
GRIMSHANK *enters from the shop. He wears a mayoral hat and chain over a striped butcher's smock*)

Act I STORY OF JACK AND THE BEANSTALK 3

GRIMSHANK. Now then, what's all this? Three cheers for the Mayor? Much obliged, lads and lasses.
1ST CHILD. We weren't cheering you, you old gas-bag.
GRIMSHANK. Eh, what a rude little lad!
JACK. Mr Grimshank, sir.
GRIMSHANK. Alderman Grimshank, your worship.
JACK. Your worship, then. On behalf of the assembled children of Mangel-Wurzel-on-the-Wold, may I remind you that although it's nearly two years* since the Coronation, we still haven't had our Coronation treat.
CHILDREN. Shame!
GRIMSHANK. Just a minute, me lad. That's a matter for Council to decide. Tell you what, I'll bring it up at next meeting.
JACK. And when's that?
GRIMSHANK. Let's see, what date is it now?
JACK. December the twenty-third,* nineteen fifty-four.
GRIMSHANK. Right! Suppose we make it January the first, nineteen fifty-six?*

(*They all groan*)

JACK. Nineteen fifty-six?* But we can't wait till then! Can we, children?
CHILDREN. No!

(GAFFER DRIBBLEDRIP *wakes up*)

GRIMSHANK. But these things take time. We 'ave to fill in forms...
JACK. Forms? Bunkum! Look what all the other children have had! At Mildew-in-the-Marsh, maypole dances and money-boxes. At Withering-in-the-Willow, pageants and propelling pencils. At Mudcombe-on-the-Moor, lantern lectures and lollipops. But here at Mangel-Wurzel-on-the-Wold...
SIMON. Not a blood-orange!
GRIMSHANK. 'Ere, 'oo asked you to chip in?
JACK. As my impetuous friend remarks, not a blood-orange. I ask you, your Worship, why shouldn't we have our Coronation celebrations and souvenirs?
GAFFER. I 'ad mine.
JACK. Who said that?
SIMON. Old Gaffer Dribbledrip.
JACK. Oh, so you've woken up, have you, Gaffer?
GAFFER. Oo aye!
JACK. And you say you've had your treat?
GAFFER. Oo aye!
GRIMSHANK. There you are! A satisfied ratepayer!
JACK. And when was this treat?

* Keep this up-to-date.

GAFFER. I don't rightly know when it were. But they gen me a moog.
JACK. A moog?
GAFFER. Aye, a moog. Yon! (*He holds out his beer-mug*)
ALICE. Look, it's got a portrait of Miss Anna Neagle.
JACK. Why, you must be thinking of Queen Victoria's Coronation!
GAFFER. 'Appen it were. I don't rightly know.
JACK. But even you can't be as old as that. (*He takes the mug*) Ah, I thought so. They gave you this at the Golden Jubilee.
GAFFER. 'Appen they did. Any road it were a reet good moog.
JACK. But surely that was in the days of the Good Old Squire?
GAFFER. Aye, that it were. Did things proper, did t'owd Squire. I tell yer, it were a sad day for us owd uns when 'e went away.
ALICE. But where did he go—and why?
GAFFER. Now the answer to that is——
ALL. Yes?
GAFFER. —I don't rightly know. But this I do know—things ain't been the same since. Village ain't the same, folks ain't the same—why, even the animals ain't the same.
ALICE. Not even the animals?
JACK. Why, Alice, surely you know the story?
ALICE. I'm afraid I don't.
JACK. Then listen and I'll tell you.

        No. 2   SONG (JACK *and* CHORUS)

JACK.
    Unlucky was the day
    When the Squire went away
And they put up the shutters at the stately hall;
    O the villagers were sad
    For they loved him like a dad
But the animals missed him most of all.
    O the cows they never moo
    Like they always used to do,
The little pussy-cats won't miaow, miaow, miaow;
    The lambs and their mama
    Never say a single "Baa!"
And the doggies won't bark bow, wow, wow, wow!

ALL.
    O the cows, etc.

JACK.
    O the birdies never sing,
    No, not even in the Spring,
All the piggies went to market and they won't come back,
    The hens are all asleep

ACT I STORY OF JACK AND THE BEANSTALK 5

    And the chickens never cheep,
  And the little Donald Ducks won't quack, quack, quack!
    O the cows they never . . .
CHORUS (*animal noises from now on*) Moo!
JACK.
    Like they always used to do,
  The little pussy-cats won't—
CHORUS.   Miaow, miaow, miaow!
JACK.
    The lambs and their mama
    Never say a single—
CHORUS.   Baa!
JACK.
  And the doggies won't bark—
CHORUS.   Bow, wow, wow, wow!
JACK.
    O the birdies never sing,
    No, not even in the Spring,
  All the piggies went to market and they won't come back,
    The hens are all asleep
    And the chickens never—
CHORUS.   Cheep!
JACK.
  And the little Donald Ducks won't—
CHORUS.   Quack, quack, quack!

(*The* CHILDREN *imitate various animals all together. Perhaps* JACK *invites the Audience to join in a chorus repeat*)

  GRIMSHAW. Shut up, now! Stop it and behave yourselves! Eh, young Jack, wait till I see your ma. Why, here she is!

(MRS DURDEN *comes out of "The Flying Horse", hands over ears. She soon quietens the Children*)

  MRS DURDEN. Time, children, please! No music, no dancing—(*to an embracing couple*) *and* no unlawful games! Do you want me to lose me licence? Really, Mr Mayor, and you a J.P.!
  GRIMSHANK. Madam, I assure you . . .
  MRS DURDEN. I'm surprised at you, I really am—encouraging such ribaldage! Jack, what do you think you're doing? Why aren't you milking the moo-cow or titivating the tankards?
  JACK. But, Mother, I'm addressing an indignation meeting.
  MRS DURDEN. Indeed? Well, from now on you'll kindly address me. I'll give you indignation.
  GAFFER. Ye see, ma'am, we was 'aving a bit of a natter about the Good Owd Squire.
  MRS DURDEN (*softening*) About Morty! Were you really? Ah,

Morty, Morty, where are you now? (*She produces a handkerchief*)

(JACK *and* ALICE *confer aside with the* CHILDREN)

SIMON. Dead as a doornail!

MRS DURDEN. He isn't, I know he isn't! Only the night before he disappeared, he promised me that some day I should be his blushing bride.

GRIMSHANK. But that was forty years ago!

MRS DURDEN. What does that matter? I can still blush beautifully. Look at me now!

GAFFER. That ain't blushin'. That's blood-pressure!

MRS DURDEN. Go away, you horrid old man!

GRIMSHANK. Why don't you forget the Squire and make the best o' me?

MRS DURDEN. I know you mean well. But Mother always warned me that it was a mistake for a girl to marry beneath her class.

GRIMSHANK. What about your late lamented? 'E was a butcher, too.

MRS DURDEN (*majestically*) Durden was in the wholesale.

GRIMSHANK. Well, I'll be . . .

MRS DURDEN. Careful, now! I warn you I won't have no language.

(*The* CHILDREN *exit, waving good-bye to Jack and Alice.* JACK *approaches Grimshank*)

JACK. Your worship, I have to present you with an ultimatum.

GRIMSHANK. And what might that be when it's at home?

JACK. No more school until we get our Coronation treat.

GRIMSHANK. It's—why, it's insupertibordinance!

JACK. Well, those are our terms. And we'll give you ten minutes to consider them. Come along, Alice, let's go and fetch Maisie.

(JACK *and* ALICE *exit*)

GAFFER. Reckon they all want a moog.

GRIMSHANK. Well, they needn't think I'm one. Coronation treat my foot!

MRS DURDEN. But why not? If Morty were here he'd do the thing properly.

GAFFER. That 'e would, ma'am. T'owd Squire would ha' roasted a hox 'ole.

MRS DURDEN. Indeed? And what, may I ask, is a hoxole?

SIMON. What he means is a whole ox.

GAFFER. Wot I said—a hoxole.

GRIMSHANK. I might manage a bit o' tripe or a string o' sausages. But as for a hox . . .

GAFFER. 'Ole.

Act I   STORY OF JACK AND THE BEANSTALK

GRIMSHANK. An' very nice, too—but who's to pay for it? There isn't the money about these days—and what there is don't come our way.
MRS DURDEN. Too true! Why, I haven't had a double let since the Americans went home. I don't know why it is, but the world seems to have quite forgotten this lovely village. Nobody ever comes to Mangel-Wurzel-on-the-Wold.

No. 3   SONG: MANGEL-WURZEL (MRS DURDEN, GRIMSHANK, GAFFER and SIMON)

MRS DURDEN.
 Nobody ever visits Mangel-Wurzel,
 Delightful Mangel-Wurzel-on-the-Wold:
  Not a tourist comes to seek
  Our gasometer unique,
 Our post-office where paraffin is sold:
 We've an interesting semi-Tudor tea-shop
 Reputed to be nearly two years old,
  And it's really quite absurd
  That you haven't even heard
 Of lovely Mangel-Wurzel-on-the-Wold.
CHORUS.
  Yes, it's really quite absurd
  That you haven't even heard
 Of lovely Mangel-Wurzel-on-the-Wold.
MRS DURDEN.
 There's some early Norman carving in St Swithin's
 Where naughty little Norman carved his name;
  Over yonder, Good Queen Bess
  Lost her Coronation dress
 In the middle of the pageant—what a shame!
 The Vicar said, "Ah, this must be Godiva!
 Intrepid girl—I trust she won't catch cold":
  Little things like that, you know,
  Help to make the party go
 At merry Mangel-Wurzel-on-the-Wold.
CHORUS.
  Little things like that, you know,
  Help to make the party go
 At merry Mangel-Wurzel-on-the-Wold.
MRS DURDEN.
 Our catering is never recommended
 By Bon Viveur or by the R.A.C.:
  Since the Cyclists' Touring Club
  Warned its members off the pub
 Nobody's ever tried a Dainty Tea:
 Yes, in spite of our exhilarating climate,

In spite of our attractions manifold
    For some reason far from clear
    Not a guide or gazetteer
Will mention Mangel-Wurzel-on-the-Wold.

CHORUS.
    For some reason far from clear,
  etc.

MRS DURDEN.
  Why spend your summer holidays at Salford?*
  We'd make you welcome as the flowers in May:
    Though it's true we've never been
    In Country Magazine
  We'd really love to see you Down Our Way:
  But the visitor we're eagerly awaiting,
  Who's definitely worth his weight in gold
    Is the enterprising chap
    Who can put upon the map
  Enchanting Mangel-Wurzel-on-the-Wold.

CHORUS.
  Yes, we're looking for the chap
  Who can put upon the map

GAFFER.
  'Istoric Mangel-Wurzel,

MRS DURDEN.
  Romantic Mangel-Wurzel,

GRIMSHANK.
  Progressive Mangel-Wurzel,

SIMON.
  Revolting Mangel-Wurzel,

ALL. Revolting Mangel-Wurzel-on-the-Wold!

(DURDEN *and* GRIMSHANK *dance off into* "*The Flying Horse*". SIMON *tries to follow but the door closes in his face.* GAFFER *offers him a pull at his mug.*

GAFFER *and* SIMON *exit together.*

JACK *and* ALICE *enter steering* MAISIE *the cow—a temperamental animal with—if possible—a wistful expression. The* CHILDREN *follow.* JACK *carries a pail*)

No. 4a CHORUS (CHILDREN)

CHILDREN. Moo-cow, Moo-cow, any milk to-day?
  Spare us a little drop of pure Grade A:
  Bread-and-jam and a piece of cake
  Go down better with a nice milk shake,
  Plain or malted and all full cream,
  That's the stuff for the football team!

* Vary as desired.

(MRS DURDEN *enters from* "*The Flying Horse*", *carrying a jug.* MAISIE *rears and sulks*)

MRS DURDEN. Milk below—oo! Come along, Maisie! Come to mother, there's a nice moo-cow!
1ST CHILD. Why, the pail's empty!
MRS DURDEN. So it is! What's the meaning of this?
JACK. I'm sorry, but Maisie isn't feeling at all well. I'm afraid she won't give us any milk today.
MRS DURDEN. No milk? Nonsense! It only needs the touch of experience. Come here, you temperamental animal! That's right, children, you hold her while I demonstrate.

(*The* CHILDREN *hold Maisie while* MRS DURDEN *operates her tail like a beer-pump, holding the jug under her*)

Last orders, please! Come along now, drink up! (*She looks at the jug, wipes imaginary froth*) And what for you, sir? Half and half? Thank you. (*She moves the jug from side to side*) Dear me, not much of a head on that! Never mind—all hands to the pumps!

(*She slaps* MAISIE *who rears and kicks her over. The* CHILDREN *laugh*)

Look what you've done, you quarrelsome quadruped! I've a good mind to sell you to the butcher—and you can put that in your cud and chew it!

(MAISIE *cowers*)

JACK. Mother, what a dreadful thing to say—even though you don't mean it.
MRS DURDEN. Don't I indeed? What's the use of a milkless mooless moo-cow—except to make a string of seamless sausages?
JACK. Now you've really hurt her feelings.
ALICE. Why, she's trembling. There, didums.

(MAISIE *noses Mrs Durden*)

MRS DURDEN. Help! Go away, you incorrigible cow!
JACK. She's only trying to say she's sorry.

(MAISIE *rubs round Mrs Durden*)

MRS DURDEN. It's no use trying to get round me.

(GRIMSHANK *and the* GAFFER *enter. The* GAFFER *now wears a town-crier's hat and carries a handbell. He mounts the bench*)

GAFFER (*ringing the bell*) Oyez! Oyez! Oyez!
CHILDREN. O no! O no! O no! O no!
GAFFER. I sez oyez! I crave silence for 'Is Worship the Mayor, as 'as a himportant hannouncement to make.

(*Ironic cheers.* GRIMSHANK *replaces* GAFFER *on the bench*)

GRIMSHANK. Ladies and gentlemen, I 'ave no intention of making a speech.

(*They all sit down with shrugs of resignation*)

I just want to tell you that this here village will have a slap-up Coronation treat at my expense——

(*Cheers*)

—next time we 'ave the pleasure of a visit from a genuine tourist.

(*Groans*)

Sorry, but that's the best I can do.

MRS DURDEN. But nobody ever visits Mangel-Wurzel!

GRIMSHANK. Aye, we know all about that. But wireless says the countryside's opening up . . .

MRS DURDEN. And we're closing down.

GRIMSHANK. 'Ave patience, can't you? 'Oo knows what may 'appen in a year or two?

JACK. A year or two? But we can't wait till then—can we, children?

CHILDREN. No!

GRIMSHANK. Order! I now declare this bazaar open.

(*Boos*)

I mean, I now declare this meetin' closed.

(*More boos as he gets off the bench.*
SIMON *enters up* R. *He has a rapt expression*)

SIMON. I seen her I say!
 I seen her I say!
 She's crossing the meadow and coming this way!
JACK. But who have you seen?
ALICE. O what can he mean?
SIMON. A lovely young lady as grand as a queen!
ALL (*tapping their foreheads*)
 Did you hear what he said?
 Now don't be misled,
 I fear this young fellow is weak in the head.
SIMON. You'd better be wary,
 Aye, better be wary,
 And mind how you treat her—because she's a fairy!
ALL. A fairy? A fairy?
 He says she's a fairy!
SIMON (*peering*)
 She's turned down the lane and she's passing the
 dairy.

ACT I   STORY OF JACK AND THE BEANSTALK

JACK (*peering*)
    A lady I see
    But no fairy is she
    No immortal who dwells
    Amid grottoes and dells,
        But a fair ballerina from far Sadler's Wells.

ALL.   It's a fair ballerina from far Sadler's Wells.

JACK.   See her trip down the street
    On such delicate feet—
        Why, children, we're saved—we shall all get our treat!
    Come along—give three cheers,
    For that lady, my dears,
        Is clearly a tourist, the first one for years!

ALL.   A tourist—hooray!
    What a wonderful day!
        We'll all have our treat and the Mayor will pay!

GRIMSHANK. Here, what's that you say?

ALL.   The Mayor will pay!

GRIMSHANK. This wants looking into—get out of my way!

(*The* BEANSTALK FAIRY *enters*)

BEANSTALK FAIRY.
    Good morning, all. I fear there's some confusion—
    I must apologize for this intrusion.

GRIMSHANK. Not a bit of it, Miss—er—Miss . . .

MRS DURDEN. Madame Markova*, I presume?

BEANSTALK FAIRY.
    Your worship flatters me—I make no claim
    To Sadler's Wells or Covent Garden fame:
    I meant to spend the morning with a friend
    I haven't seen for years in Ponders End:
    Now, by miscalculation unforeseen,
    Instead I find myself in Golders Green.

GRIMSHANK. Golders Green? But that's miles away—a ten-penny bus fare! This is Mangel-Wurzel-on-the-Wold.

MRS DURDEN. And this is *The Flying Horse*. Why not come in and try our speciality—Aunt Martha's Home-made Cottage Pie?

BEANSTALK FAIRY.
    Please tell Aunt Martha that I'd love to try it:
    I just adore a wholesome country diet.

    * Or other well-known ballerina.

MRS DURDEN (*calling through the door*) Maggie! Open a small tin of Aunt Martha's Home-made Cottage Pie!
JACK. Just a moment, lady. Before you go to lunch, won't you please tell us who you are?
BEANSTALK FAIRY.
    Young man, whoever most you wish to see
    Be sure that you behold her now in me.
JACK. Does that mean—you really are a tourist?
BEANSTALK FAIRY.
    I am indeed—as presently you'll find—
    A tourist of a rather special kind.

(*The* FAIRY *goes into* "*The Flying Horse*" *with* MRS DURDEN)

JACK. Hear that, Mr Mayor? Now what about our treat?
CHILDREN. Yes—what about it?
GRIMSHANK. All right, kids—you win. Come back in ten minutes and I'll see what I can do.
CHILDREN. Hooray!

(GRIMSHANK *goes into* "*The Flying Horse*". *The* CHILDREN *and* SIMON, *with* MAISIE, *go off singing*)

    No. 4b CHORUS: *Repeat of No. 1* (CHILDREN)
        Girls and boys come out to play:
        Lots of fun we'll have today;
        Lots of lovely things to eat
        At our Coronation treat!

(GAFFER *takes his seat on the bench*) .

ALICE. Why does that lady always speak in rhyme
       Just like a fairy in a pahtomime?
JACK. Perhaps a television parlour game—
      That's curious! We're doing just the same!
ALICE. Why, so we are! There's simply nothing to it.
       Fancy, we're poets and we never knew it.
JACK. I do believe you're right. Our verse may not
      Resemble that of Mr Eliot—
      It rhymes and scans—but all the same, it's verse:
      On greeting cards I've read a good deal worse.
      Are we the only ones? Or can it be . . .
GAFFER. 'Ark at them two a-sayin' poetree!
ALICE. Did you hear that? The Gaffer's made a rhyme!
GAFFER. Nay, you'll none catch me wastin' of me time!
        I nivver 'ad no 'ead for rhymes an' such:
        To me they sounds like proper double-Dutch.

Act I STORY OF JACK AND THE BEANSTALK

(MRS DURDEN *comes out of "The Flying Horse" and takes the mug from Gaffer*)

ALICE.   You see? It must be magic! I declare
           Today there's magic in the very air!

MRS DURDEN.
           There's many a slip, they say, 'twixt cup and lip—
           That certainly applies to Dribbledrip!

JACK.   Alice, my dear, I'm certain you are right—
           Why, even mother's starting to recite!

MRS DURDEN.
           What, me? Such poppycock and fiddlesticks!
           I can't be bothered with your silly tricks—
           Good gracious, now you've got me at it, too!
           There, that's enough now, run along with you!

(MRS DURDEN *goes into "The Flying Horse"*)

ALICE.   Look how amazement on thy mother sits!

JACK.   A line Shakespearean that truly fits
           A situation curious and exciting:
           Let's find our friends and see what they're reciting!

(ALICE *and* JACK *go off* R.
GRIMSHANK *and* MRS DURDEN *come out of "The Flying Horse"*)

MRS DURDEN.
           Well, there it is. Whatever you may say
           The boys and girls will have to have their way.
           You've promised them their treat—no doubt about it
           You'll never get them back to school without it.

GRIMSHANK.
           All very well for you—I've got to fill
           And furthermore to foot the blooming bill:
           They all expect a proper slap-up treat
           With fireworks, a galler and a feet . . .

MRS DURDEN.
           Surely you mean a gahlah and a fête?

(GAFFER *rises and gesticulates*)

GRIMSHANK.
           Cut out the la-di-da! (*To Gaffer*) What is it, mate?

GAFFER.   Why don't you roast a hox 'ole like the Squire?

GRIMSHANK.
           Trust you to put the fat well in the fire!

(MAISIE *wanders in*)

GAFFER.   Nay, why not give 'em in the good owd fashion
           That little bit of hextra hoff the ration?
GRIMSHANK.
           I've got no ox to roast...
MRS DURDEN.   But I've a cow!
           Come here, nice Maisie! Come to mother, now!
           She hasn't any milk and doesn't moo—
           She's good for nothing but an Irish stew:
           I'll sell her to you cheap.
GRIMSHANK.   How much?
MRS DURDEN.   Five bob.
GRIMSHANK.
           Done! Come here, Maisie—why, you're just the job!
           (*He fetches a carving-knife from the shop and chases Maisie*)

(JACK *enters followed by* ALICE *and the* CHILDREN)

JACK.   Leave her alone! I say you shall not touch her!
           She's mine! You let her be, you beastly butcher!
GRIMSHANK (*catching Maisie*)
           Children, behold your Coronation treat!
GAFFER.   Aye, she'll be very tasty, very sweet!

No. 5a CHORUS (CHILDREN)

Good-bye, Maisie!
Good-bye, Maisie!
Good-bye, Maisie!
We're going to eat you now!
See the butcher whet his knife
Whet his knife!
Whet his knife!
He's about to take her life,
Pity the poor old cow!

No. 5b ENSEMBLE (JACK, GRIMSHANK, MRS DURDEN, GAFFER *and* CHILDREN)

JACK.   Who claims my cow?
GRIMSHANK.   I, says the Mayor,
              Preparin' to slay 'er:
              I claim your cow.
CHILDREN.   All the kids of the village are a-piping of the eye
              For to hear that the poor old cow must die,
              For to hear that the poor old cow must die!

JACK.	Who'll dare to roast her?
MRS DURDEN.	I'm no idle boaster, And with my electric toaster, I'll dare to roast her!
CHILDREN.	All the kids, etc.
JACK.	Who'll dare to eat her?
GAFFER.	I, says the Owd Un, With me one tooth—a gowd un— I'll dare to eat her!
CHILDREN.	All the kids, etc.
GRIMSHANK.	Cheer up, you kids, we'll have some lovely gravy, The kind they give the Army and the Navy.
JACK.	Please, Mr Mayor, put away your knife: O spare a humble and a blameless life!
GRIMSHANK.	Nay, stand aside, ungrateful lad and daughter! She's mine, I tell you!
JACK.	Not until you've caught her!

(*There is a scuffle.*
The BEANSTALK FAIRY *comes out of "The Flying Horse"*)

BEANSTALK FAIRY.	Shame on you all, I say! Are you barbarians?
GRIMSHANK.	No, miss—but neither are we vegetarians.
GAFFER.	We want our bit of hextra hoff the ration!
BEANSTALK FAIRY.	Then why not claim it in true Spanish fashion?
JACK.	Why not? Let's have a bull-fight! Off you go, El toro Maisie and El Grimshanko!
GRIMSHANK.	What, her a bull and me a toreador? Mind you, I've never done this kind of thing before. Still, to oblige you, miss, I'll have a bash And do me best to cut a Spanish dash.

No. 6a INCIDENTAL MUSIC

(*While this is played* GRIMSHANK *is handed a red curtain on a rod. He salutes* MRS DURDEN *who has donned a mantilla, produced a fan and put a rose between her teeth. The others form a ring.* MAISIE *wakes up and paws the ground. During the chorus a burlesque bull-fight takes place*)

16 STORY OF JACK AND THE BEANSTALK   ACT I

No. 6b CHORUS (JACK, ALICE, GAFFER, SIMON *and* CHILDREN)
ALL. Now, Maisie Moo-cow, put your stuff across,
     Give him a toss!
     Show you're the boss!
     Do remember that he'll kill you if he can,
     That unkind butcher man,
     He'll kill you if he can,
     That butcher man,
     He'll kill you if he can!

No. 6c TANGO

(MAISIE *and* GRIMSHANK *tango together, while* MRS DURDEN *does a "pas seul".* MAISIE *steals her rose. During repeat of chorus* MAISIE *wins the fight and puts everyone to flight except* JACK, ALICE *and the* BEANSTALK FAIRY. JACK *and* ALICE *embrace* MAISIE)

JACK. O gallant Maisie, you have won the day!
      Thank you so much, Miss—what name shall I say?

(MAISIE *wanders off*)

BEANSTALK FAIRY.
      No name at all—you are too curious:
      And now it's time for me to catch my bus.

JACK. O what a pity! Must you really go?

BEANSTALK FAIRY.
      Yes, I'm afraid I really must, although
      Before I do I certainly must pay
      For the delicious lunch I had today.
      Here, take this purse, young man.

ALICE (*aside*)   How very strange!

JACK. I'm sorry, but I haven't any change.

BEANSTALK FAIRY.
      Keep it—and may it furnish wealth untold
      To you and Mangel-Wurzel-on-the-Wold.

(*The* BEANSTALK FAIRY *gives him the purse and vanishes*)

JACK. Thank you—but, miss, I'm sure there's far too much! Alice, just feel how heavy the purse is.

ALICE. Why have you stopped talking poetry?

JACK. Have I? Are you sure?

ALICE. Of course.

JACK. And so have you. Perhaps if we asked the lady . . . Why, where is she?

ALICE. She's—why, she's gone.

JACK. Gone? But she was here only a moment ago. She can't be far away.

ALICE. I suppose she can't—that is, not unless . . . (*She pauses*)

JACK. Unless what?
ALICE. O, Jack, suppose Simple Simon was right after all!
JACK. You mean that the lady was really . . . ? But that's impossible! There just aren't any fairies nowadays. Everybody knows that.
ALICE. I'm not so sure. Perhaps that's a fairy purse.
JACK. It looks real—it feels real—it *is* real. And full of extra hard currency. Probably Spanish doubloons . . .
ALICE. How romantic!
JACK. Or American dollars!
ALICE. How even more romantic! Do open it and see!

(GRIMSHANK *and* MRS DURDEN *enter*)

GRIMSHANK. Where's that confounded cow?
MRS DURDEN. And where's that bally ballerina?
ALICE. Maisie's in the meadow so you're quite safe.
JACK. And the lady's just caught her bus to Ponders End.
ALICE (*aside*) I wonder!
GRIMSHANK. What? Calls herself a tourist? Why, she's nowt but a half-day tripper!
JACK. She left this to pay for her lunch.
MRS DURDEN. A purse, eh? Give it to me. I hope she's remembered the service charge and the staff fund and a little something for the waitress. (*She opens the purse*)
JACK. I'm sure she has. It's chock full of money.
MRS DURDEN (*taking out the beans*) Money? Money? Just look at this! Dished, diddled and done!
GRIMSHANK. Why, these are nobbut common beans!
ALICE. Beans? But they can't be!
MRS DURDEN. Can't they? Just look at them!
ALICE. And we thought they were doubloons and dollars!
MRS DURDEN. I might have known! They're all the same, these theatricals. This week at Nottingham Playhouse,* next week at Skegness Arcadia.* Pretending to be glamour girls and they haven't got a bean.
JACK. This lady had—a whole bag of them.
MRS DURDEN. What do I want with a bag of beans?
JACK. At least you can have them on toast.
MRS DURDEN. I suppose you think you're having me on toast. Bah! That's what I think of your beans! (*She throws them into the well*) And as for you, young man—take, that, and that, and that! (*She beats Jack*)
ALICE. It wasn't his fault, Mrs Durden—it really wasn't.
GRIMSHANK. And that'll be enough from you, me lass. (*Pulling her towards the shop*) Off to bed with you, and don't let me catch you with that good-for-nothing young . . .

* Substitute your own and another local theatre.

MRS DURDEN (*releasing Jack*) Don't you dare call my boy a good-for-nothing! You keep your eye on that fast little madam!
GRIMSHANK (*releasing Alice*) Did I hear you call my daughter a fast little madam?
MRS DURDEN. You certainly did. It's girls like her that make boys like him leave mothers like me.

(*While they quarrel* JACK *and* ALICE *steal off hand in hand.* MAISIE *wanders in unobserved*)

GRIMSHANK. If I had a mother like you I wouldn't leave her.
MRS DURDEN. Oh, wouldn't you?
GRIMSHANK. Not me. I'm far too humane.
MRS DURDEN. Indeed?
GRIMSHANK. That's why I'd use a humane killer.
MRS DURDEN. Oh, so you'd kill your own mother? I suppose you'd kill the whole family?
GRIMSHANK. Well, I am a family butcher.
MRS DURDEN. Call yourself a butcher? What about that tripe you sent me?
GRIMSHANK. What's wrong with my tripe?
MRS DURDEN. It's simply offal. Oo, that was a good one!

(*She slaps him and turns away to laugh.*
GRIMSHANK *sees Maisie and runs off in alarm.* MAISIE *nudges* MRS DURDEN, *who wriggles coquettishly*)

MRS DURDEN. Now then, go along with you. I don't allow no familiarity on or off the premises.

(MAISIE *nudges her again*)

Naughty, naughty! Want me to forgive you, I suppose?

(MAISIE *butts her*)

Stop it, you great big he-man you! My Humphrey Bogart! (*She turns and sees Maisie*) Help! Murder!

(MAISIE *chases* MRS DURDEN *off. The scene darkens to moonlight, and lights come up in the windows.*
The BEANSTALK FAIRY *enters*)

BEANSTALK FAIRY.
  Now the shades of night enfold
  Mangel-Wurzel-on-the-Wold:
  Hither from my home afar
  Under an auspicious star
  I invisible return
  More of my young friends to learn.
  Now to weave a spell astounding
  While the witching hour is sounding.

MRS DURDEN (*within*) Time, gentlemen, please!
(SIMON *and* GAFFER *come out of* "*The Flying Horse*" *and cross* R)
SIMON.   I tell you that I seen 'er wand and wings!
GAFFER. And I tell you that there ain't no such things!
SIMON.   I seen her plain as plain—aye, you can scoff!
GAFFER. You 'ave a good night's rest an' sleep it off.
(SIMON *goes into the shop*)
GAFFER. The lad's that daft 'e makes yer proper vexed!
         Fairies in Mangel-Wurzel! Eh, wot next!
(GAFFER *goes off*)
BEANSTALK FAIRY.
         Sometimes, old man, a simpleton descries
         Things undiscovered by the worldly-wise:
         But what has happened to my lovers twain—
         The butcher's daughter and her stripling swain?
         Ah, here they come—Jack and his Alice dear:
         Their honied conference I'll overhear.
(JACK *and* ALICE *enter. They go to the shop door*)
JACK.   Must you go in? It's hardly ten o'clock:
         It was the pussy-cat and not the owl
         That made a fearful noise in yonder tree.
ALICE.   It was the owl and not the pussy-cat:
         The pubs are turning out, and cross papa
         Is switching off the television play.
         I would not for the world he found you here.
JACK.   We have the dark to hide us from his eyes.
ALICE.   Do you love me? I know you will say yes.
(*They kiss*)
BEANSTALK FAIRY.
         With sentimental tears my eyes are wet!
         Echo of Romeo! Shade of Juliet!
GRIMSHANK (*within*)
         Alice, where art thou?
ALICE.   Listen, there's father calling! I must go!
         I'm coming, Father! Just a moment, Jack:
         Wait by the window, dear, and I'll be back.
(ALICE *exits into the shop*)
JACK.   O what an absolutely smashing night!
         At last the further outlook's really bright;
         You see, we're fed up with the way they treat us:

Our parents only bullyrag and beat us:
We think it's high time that we emigrated
To some place where we'll be appreciated;
And so our plans are well and truly laid,
Our careful calculations duly made:
You've guessed it—we've resolved to run away!
We're off tomorrow at the break of day
To—oh, we'll follow any path inviting
And stop at—any place that seems exciting,
And there we'll—do whatever suits us best—
Something superb, like climbing Everest!

(*He goes to the window*)

BEANSTALK FAIRY.
This expedition's incompletely planned:
It's evidently time I took a hand:
What foolish vows his young ambition makes!
But soft—what light through yonder window breaks?

(ALICE *appears with a lamp at the upper window*)

ALICE. Three words, dear Jack, then I must say good night:
Tomorrow, I'll be ready as I promised
To follow you, my dear, through all the world.

GRIMSHANK (*within*) Alice!
ALICE. I'm coming, Father. (*To Jack*) When must I be ready?
GRIMSHANK (*within*) Alice!
ALICE. In a moment!
JACK. I'll come and fetch you at the crack of dawn.
ALICE. Till dawn, then. How I wish it were tomorrow!
JACK. Good night, dear Alice. Parting is such sweet sorrow!

(ALICE *withdraws*)

Eight hours to dawn! What ever shall I do from now to then?
BEANSTALK FAIRY. Good evening.
JACK. Why, it's you! What are you up to? Why have you come back?
BEANSTALK FAIRY.
You don't seem very pleased to see me, Jack.

JACK. Don't I? No wonder! Madam, you forget
The way you cheated me when last we met.
Why are you laughing? Do you think it's funny
To give a fellow beans instead of money?

BEANSTALK FAIRY.
My boy, those beans are worth their weight in gold
To you and Mangel-Wurzel-on-the-Wold.

Act I STORY OF JACK AND THE BEANSTALK

JACK.   Tell me another.
BEANSTALK FAIRY.   What, my word you're doubting?
Behold your beans already quickly sprouting!
Where they by hand improvident were cast.
JACK.   Why, so they are! I say, they're growing fast!
BEANSTALK FAIRY.
Not nearly fast enough! Such vegetation
Requires assistance from an incantation.
JACK.   An incantation? But that's magic! Why,
Then you must be . . .
BEANSTALK FAIRY.   The Beanstalk Fairy I!
JACK.   Then Simple Simon *was* right after all.
BEANSTALK FAIRY.
Just wait until you see my beanstalk tall.
JACK.   I say, I'm sorry that I've been so dumb!
BEANSTALK FAIRY.
Don't mention it! My dear assistants, come
And let us give our lecture-demonstration
On raising Magic Beans by Incantation!

(*The Beanstalk is seen rising from the well.*
FAIRIES *enter and dance round it, carrying tiny watering-cans*)

No. 7   DUET (JACK *and* BEANSTALK FAIRY)

BEANSTALK FAIRY.
    If you would know
    How to grow
Magical plant so tall and greeny,
    This is the way—
    After me say,
"Eeny, meeny, greeny beany!"
BOTH.   "Eeny meeny teeny weeny greeny beany, beany!"
    Eeny meeny beany O!
    This is the way to gather, you know,
      Medals a score
      And cups galore
    At the Horticultural Show.
JACK.   Tall as a tree,
    As you can see,
Science is wise but magic wiser.
    Who could go wrong,
    Singing a song?
What an effective fertilizer!

BOTH. As you see, a most effective fairy fertilizer.
Eeny meeny beany O!
Round the Beanstalk, heel and toe:
Hardly can $\left\{{I \atop he}\right\}$
Believe $\left\{{my \atop his}\right\}$ eyes;
Soon it will surely reach the skies!

(*As the song ends the* FAIRIES *dance off. Dawn breaks. The Beanstalk now appears full grown*)

JACK. O what amazing beans!
BEANSTALK FAIRY. And yet, you know,
Last year we had an even better show.

(ALICE *comes out of the shop, wearing a haversack*)

But see, the sun is up—
ALICE. And so am I!
Why, what is this ascending to the sky?
BEANSTALK FAIRY.
A living ladder, an enchanted stair
To frowning castle, fearful giant's lair
Where treasure lies, for him who has the wit
And courage to possess himself of it.
JACK. I've shinned up lots of fruit-trees in my time:
For golden fruit I'd chance a stiffer climb.
ALICE. Not without me you won't.
JACK. But, Alice, dear,
This is man's work. How could I take you near
A fearsome giant? The idea's absurd!
ALICE. You promised me—you gave your solemn word!
Besides, I'm jolly good at climbing trees.
O, won't you let me be your Sherpa, please?
JACK. All right, you win!
ALICE. O thank you, darling Jack!
JACK. Did you bring sandwiches?
ALICE. They're in my pack.
JACK. Then we are ready!
BEANSTALK FAIRY. May you both be lucky
As you are young, adventurous and plucky!
JACK. Come on, my Sherpa, up the sylvan stair:
Fairy, farewell—and giant grim, beware!

Quick CURTAIN *rising on tableau—*MAISIE *looking wistfully up the Beanstalk, while* GRIMSHANK, GAFFER, MRS DURDEN *and* SIMPLE SIMON *peer out of the windows. The* GAFFER *is looking through a bent telescope.*

CURTAIN

ACT II

SCENE—*Inside the Giant's Castle.*

It is a large bare room in pseudo-Gothic. There is a recess up R screened by a curtain bearing a notice "Private". Up LC is a large window with a sky-cloth behind. Down R is a bench; up L, a chest on which sits the Magic Hen. There is a door L leading to a staircase. A chair and table stand C.

When the CURTAIN *rises,* MR *and* MRS CROAKER *enter* L. *They are a fairy version of elderly Victorian domestic servants, with tiny wings.* Croaker *is an urbane, easy-going villain kept up to scratch by Mrs Croaker, who has the manner of an old-style tragedy queen.* CROAKER *is carrying a tea-tray. He puts it on the table and opens the window.*

MRS CROAKER. Now the horrid night is past;
Dreadful day has dawned at last;
Bat and owl do homeward fly;
Various voices call from high,
Voices moaning piteouslee—

CROAKER. "Where's our early morning tea?"

MRS CROAKER. Now the blindworm, disinterred,
Tries to dodge the early bird;
Now the wretch from bed of woe,
Haggard, laggard, limp and low,
Totters down to find his fate—

CROAKER. Bacon burned and breakfast late.

MRS CROAKER. Doom, destruction, dire disaster
Rack and wreck our Giant master,
Thundering with rage infernal—

CROAKER. "Nothing in the *Fairy Journal!*"

MRS CROAKER. Is that the morning paper, Archibald?

CROAKER. It is indubitably, Ermyntrude.

MRS CROAKER. Before you take it to the Giant, see
If it contains our small advertisement
In Situations Wanted—Household Staff.

CROAKER. I cannot find it, 'tis not in the column.
Where are my glasses?

MRS CROAKER. O infirm of optic,
Give me the paper. Ah yes, here it is—
A little masterpiece of Fairy prose.

CROAKER. As I remember, this is how it goes . . .

No. 8 DUET (CROAKER *and* MRS CROAKER)

CROAKER.	A highly-respectable married couple—
MRS CROAKER.	Both of unblemished reputation,
CROAKER.	Now getting on but extremely supple—
MRS CROAKER.	Tired of our present situation.
CROAKER.	We're feeling a sense of deep frustration,
	And that is why
	The wife and I—
MRS CROAKER.	Seek an alternative occupation.

(*They dance*)

CROAKER. This is our favourite recreation.

MRS CROAKER.	We're partly human and partly fairy—
CROAKER.	As you can guess from our faun-like faces—
MRS CROAKER.	Skilful in matters culinary—
CROAKER.	We never presume and we know our places.
MRS CROAKER.	We make spaghetti from old shoe-laces,
	Delicious stew
	From snails and glue—
CROAKER.	Cabinet puddings from packing-cases.

(*They dance*)

Notice we never neglect the graces.

For family life we've a special liking,
MRS CROAKER.	A childless home we've always hated,
CROAKER.	Our way with the children is really striking,
MRS CROAKER.	We happen to know it's appreciated.
CROAKER.	Their bones should be very finely grated—
MRS CROAKER.	And grill while fresh
	The children's flesh—
CROAKER.	It's apt to lose flavour when desiccated.

(*They dance*)

The Russians were terribly over-rated.

That strain again! It hath—

MRS CROAKER.   Enough, no more!
'Tis even lousier than it was before.
Besides, the Castle is today on view
And customers are waiting in a queue.
You tell the tale while I collect the fees.

(CROAKER *opens the door* L)

CROAKER. This way to see the castle, if you please!

(FAIRIES *enter singing, paying Mrs Croaker as they pass*)

MRS CROAKER. Pay at the desk, please, madam—two-and-six. No children, cameras or walking-sticks.

(*As they sing the* FAIRIES *dance about the room.* CROAKER *produces a lecturer's pointer*)

No. 9a CHORUS (FAIRIES)

FAIRIES. This castle is, I understand,
The oldest one in Fairyland;
It really is a great disgrace
The way that they neglect the place;
The Giant's very fierce, they say—
Of course we shan't see *him* today;
Just look out of the window, do!
Oh, isn't it a lovely view?

CROAKER. Ladies and gentlemen, I now will try
To tell you something of the history—

FAIRIES. This castle is, etc.

CROAKER. Be quiet, there, I cannot hear myself!
As I was saying, this historic castle—
Come here—sit down—keep still—I give it up!
They just aren't interested!

MRS CROAKER.   Silence there!

(*There is instant silence*)

Or you'll arouse the cruel hungry Giant.
A word from me or Mr Croaker here,
And out he'll come and eat you every one!
Continue, Archibald!

CROAKER.   Thank you, my dear.

(*To the Fairies*)

This castle hath a pleasant seat—just try it.

(*The* FAIRIES *sit on the bench. During the next speech they yawn and nod*)

Ladies and gentlemen, we now begin
Our tour of this historic man-si-on.
In this the oldest portion of the fabric
Originally built by Florimond
The First, but reconstructed by his son,
King Florimond the Second, then destroyed

	By siege and fire in the glorious reign Of Florimond the Third, later restored By Florimond the Fourth, again destroyed By Florimond the Fifth, again restored By Florimond the Sixth . . .
1ST FAIRY.	I say, old fellow, We didn't come here for a history lesson, So why not skip that ancient boring stuff And show us what we really came to see— The Magic Hen, I mean.
FAIRIES.	The Hen, the Hen!
MRS CROAKER.	Will you shut up or shall I fetch the Giant?
1ST FAIRY.	Come on now, mister, have a heart. Remember We haven't got all day.
CROAKER.	Oh, very well! As you all know, the castle's greatest treasure, Indubitably, is this Magic Hen Which lays a golden egg at nine o'clock Each morning punctually.
2ND FAIRY.	Fancy that!
CROAKER.	The curious creature was presented by The Wizard Warbusha to Florimond The Seventeenth . . .
1ST FAIRY.	Oh dear, he's off again!

(*Nine o'clock begins to strike*)

2ND FAIRY.	Listen—hooray—it's chiming nine o'clock! Time for another egg! Come on, old cock!

(*There is the sound of an egg falling in the chest*)

CROAKER.	Observe that I have nothing up my sleeve: I merely raise the latch, open the door, And presto! Here's the golden egg, hall-marked. There's no deception. Madam, would you care To examine it more closely?

(*He shows the egg round*)

MRS CROAKER.	Archibald! Be careful.
CROAKER.	That's enough now, give it back.
2ND FAIRY.	I want to take it home!
FAIRIES.	We all want one!
CROAKER (*pocketing the egg*)	Well, really! They expect a gold egg free Thrown in with half-a-crown admission fee!

	There, that's enough of that now—run away!
	Let's hear no more of golden eggs today.
1st Fairy.	Please tell us, mister, why is that marked
	"Private"?
Croaker.	Because that is the residential wing.
	The present tenant is a cruel Giant;
	With rates and taxes on the present scale
	He can't afford to keep his former state
	But occupies the ancient torture-chamber
	Converted to a nice bed-sitting-room
	With all mod. con. So keep out of his way
	And let me show you the extensive view
	From this delightful window, which commands
	The ancient frontier of our fairy realm.

(*The* Fairies *look out of the window*)

1st Fairy.	I say, do mortals live down there?
Croaker.	Indeed
	They do, but far away and out of sight.
	The Anglo-Fairyland frontier is closed
	And none may pass without a special permit
	Seldom applied for, never granted.
1st Fairy	Then
	Do mortals never come to Fairyland?
	No tourists, no commercial travellers?
Croaker.	Not even Broadway stars to top the bill.
	We are unvisited by flying saucers
	Or other interplanetary craft.
	So is our peaceful Fairyland preserved
	'Gainst infiltration and the hand of war.
1st Fairy.	Then what is that I see from earth arising?
Croaker.	From earth? Impossible!
Mrs Croaker.	Why, what is this?

(*They all peer out of the window*)

1st Fairy.	A serpent writhing upwards!
Mrs Croaker.	Let me look:
	Why, so it is! A serpent sinister,
	And on it human figures! They must be
	The spearhead of a vast invasion force.
	To arms, ye fairies! Guard the window, while
	I and my spouse hold warlike conference.
	Come, Archibald!

(*The* Croakers *whisper aside*)

1st Fairy.   Ye territorials,
            Fall in! Slope wands, and by the right, quick
               march!

                  No. 9b CHORUS (Fairies)
Fairies.   Who dares to tackle the fairies brave?
            Our foes discover an early grave;
            Courage in heart and a wand in hand.
               Ready to fight,
               Or ready to die
               For Fairyland!

(*While the* Croakers *confer the* Fairies *march round the room, then point their wands at the window*)

Croaker (*aside*) I cannot say I like this plot of yours,
            It's far too risky. If we fail—
Mrs Croaker.   We fail!
            But stick your courage up with Sellotape
            And we'll not fail.
Croaker.   Just as you say, my dear,
            Although I sometimes wish you'd never joined
            The Fairyland Shakespeare Society.
1st Fairy. Is this a serpent that I see below me?
            Why, no, it is a Beanstalk!
Fairies.   What, a Beanstalk?
1st Fairy. A magic Beanstalk, on whose branches ride
            No soldiers, but a mortal youth and maid.
Mrs Croaker. Instructed by the British Secret Service.
            I say these agents of a Foreign Power
            Must be arrested. Fairies, do your duty!
1st Fairy. Don't worry, madam, we'll take care of this!
    (*The* Beanstalk *appears outside the window with* Jack *and* Alice)
            Mortals, I call upon you to surrender!
Fairies.   Mortals, we call upon you to surrender!
Jack.   Surrender? Why, what means this show of arms,
            This martial port and preparation?
            We come in friendship.
Alice.   Yes, of course we do.
Jack.   To gentle fairies we intend no harm;
            From wicked Giant we would set you free
            And so establish true democracee.
Mrs Croaker. A tale we've heard before. Do you surrender?

JACK.　　　　Without a fight? What do you take me for?
　　　　　　One British lad is worth a dozen fairies!

(*He jumps into the room.* ALICE *follows*)

ALICE.　　　Oh, do be careful, Jack!
JACK.　　　　　　　　　　　　　　　Leave this to me!
　　　　　　Keep in the corner while I do my stuff—
　　　　　　A coward he who first cries, Hold, enough!

(JACK *tries to fight the* FAIRIES, *but they point their wands and he is forced to his knees*)

CROAKER.　　Go, attack him!
　　　　　　Crack him!
　　　　　　Whack him!
MRS CROAKER.　Needle-prick him!
　　　　　　Stick him!
　　　　　　Trick him!
CROAKER.　　Beat him!
　　　　　　Cheat him!
　　　　　　So defeat him!
BOTH.　　　Leave him bound
　　　　　　Upon the ground!
　　　　　　Let the Giant come and eat him!
　　　　　　Grab the girl and quickly bind her—
　　　　　　Let the hungry Giant find her!

(*The* FAIRIES *bind and gag* JACK *and* ALICE *with ribbons. The* 1ST FAIRY *places a foot on Jack*)

1ST FAIRY.　Well done, my gallant comrades one and all!
　　　　　　The day is ours, the foe is overthrown;
　　　　　　Be this a warning to our enemies—
　　　　　　Come the four corners of the world in arms
　　　　　　And we will shock them—naught shall make us rue
　　　　　　While fairy soldiers are as brave as you.

(*The* FAIRIES *cheer. A* VOICE *is heard from behind the curtain up* R)

VOICE (*off*)　Fe, fi, fo, fum!
　　　　　　Fairies, tremble,
　　　　　　Here I come!

(*The* FAIRIES *dash about in agitation*)

1ST FAIRY.　The Wicked Giant!
2ND FAIRY.　　　　　　　　　Help!
1ST FAIRY.　　　　　　　　　　　　　Let's run away
　　　　　　That we may live to fight another day!

(*The* FAIRIES *run off* L, *the* 1ST FAIRY *dropping his wand*)
CROAKER.   The Giant is awake! Our plot is foiled!
MRS CROAKER. Oh, no, it isn't! I will drug his posset—
CROAKER.   His what?
MRS CROAKER.   His posset—that's his morning tea—
            With Drowsy Syrup of Mandragora.

(*She produces the jar and pours some syrup into the teapot*)
            Go, push it to him underneath the curtain;
            Go on with you—what are you waiting for?

(CROAKER *pushes the tea-tray under the curtain*)

CROAKER.   He's sure to notice the peculiar taste,
            Like mingled margarine and motor-oil.
MRS CROAKER. But not until the Drowsy Syrup's passed
            His lips. One drop will send him fast asleep,
            And when he wakens——
CROAKER.   If he ever does.
MRS CROAKER. —We'll both be down the Beanstalk and away
            With Magic Hen and bags and bags of gold—
            Enough to buy a modest boarding-house
            In bracing Blackpool, famed for fairy lights.
CROAKER.   I've often thought I'd like to emigrate—
            But won't the Giant raise a hue and cry?
MRS CROAKER. By then we will have cut the Beanstalk down,
            And once again a gulf impassable
            Will yawn between the earth and Fairyland.
CROAKER.   Which means this pretty pair will have to stay
            In Fairyland for ever.
MRS CROAKER.   So they will;
            Our cruel master's sure to keep them here
            As butler-valet and cook-housekeeper
            While you and I are free and far away.
CROAKER.   And serve them right! Come on, let's go and
                pack,
            For we must leave with treasure on our back.

(*The* CROAKERS *exit* L. JACK *wriggles towards the wand, and puts his wrists to its tip. His bonds break. He tears off his gag, then frees* ALICE)

JACK.   Hooray, I'm free! This wand has done the trick!
            Hold on, dear—I'll release you in a tick.
ALICE.   Oh, Jack, let's hurry! We must get away
            Or we'll be here for ever and a day.

JACK.	What, run away and leave the Giant at
	The mercy of the proletariat?
VOICE (*off*)	What, think'st thou then
	To beard the lion in his den,
	The Giant in his hall?
	And hopest thou hence unscathed to go?
	No, by Saint Bunce of Balham*, no!
ALICE.	I told you so! The Giant's wide awake
	And on the rampage! Darling, for my sake
	Do let's go home!
JACK.	My duty bids me stay.
ALICE.	It doesn't, dear—it bids you run away.
JACK.	O shall I face the fearful Giant's fury
	Or leave him to his fate? Let's ask the jury!
	Please, children, tell your hero what to do:
	The choice I leave entirely to you:
	Shall I find out what stuff the Giant's made of?
	They answer yes!
ALICE.	That's what I was afraid of.
JACK.	If you're afraid, go home and leave me to
	Conduct alone this ticklish interview.
ALICE.	What an idea! I wouldn't dream of it.
	I am not really frightened, not a bit.

(JACK *tiptoes towards the curtain*)

JACK.	Now for it, then.
ALICE.	O do be careful, dear.
JACK.	Stand back, and I'll protect you, never fear.
VOICE (*off*)	It is the hungry Giant's joy
	To smell the blood of a British boy:
	He grinds his teeth, he smacks his lips,
	And thinks of toasted boy-and-chips.
JACK.	O what an ass I was to leave behind
	My trusty Dan Dare space-gun!
ALICE.	Never mind;
	Remember, bark is often worse than bite.
	Do hurry up, or we shall be all night.
JACK.	Why, can't you see I'm longing for the tussle?
	I merely pause to—well, to flex my muscle.
VOICE (*off*)	Beware, beware of Giant Grim!

* Make him a local saint.

JACK. Help!
ALICE. Now's your chance to tackle him!

(*The* VOICE *grows slower and deeper like a record running down—which indeed it is*)

VOICE (*off*) Blood is the only food for hmmmmmmmmmm.

(JACK *pulls back the curtain to reveal* SIR MORTIMER MORTIBOY *winding up an ancient horn gramophone. Sir Mortimer is a very old Victorian gentleman. He wears a dressing-gown over dark trousers and cravat. A monocle dangles from his breast.* SIR MORTIMER *puts the monocle into his eye and stares at Alice*)

SIR MORTIMER. Begad! A white woman!
ALICE. Why, I believe he's English!
SIR MORTIMER (*severely*) Young lady, I am her Britannic Majesty's Ambassador to the Court of Fairyland.
JACK. Our own Ambassador! Just fancy that!
We've found another missing diplomat.
SIR MORTIMER. Look here, young feller. You're British, aren't you?
JACK. Of course, your Excellency, every bit,
And so is Alice.
ALICE. And we're proud of it.
SIR MORTIMER. Well then, talk English, there's a good chap.
JACK. You mean—you don't like the fairy rhyming language?
SIR MORTIMER. Can't stand it. All rhyme and no reason. Beastly swot, these records.
ALICE (*reading the record label*) "Fairy Dialects for Beginners. Learn While You Listen." So that's what you were doing!
SIR MORTIMER. You know what natives are. Will jabber at you in their own dashed lingo. Begad, it's good to meet a Britisher!
JACK. That's what we think.
ALICE. You see, your Excellency, we thought you were a Wicked Giant.
SIR MORTIMER. Oh, you did, did you? Well, can't say I blame you. It's these fairy cartoonists. Pretend all upper-class Britishers are Wicked Giants.
JACK. How very misleading!
SIR MORTIMER. Government orders. Propaganda. Who'd be a diplomat these days? But look here, where did you two spring from?
JACK. I brought Alice up the Beanstalk.
SIR MORTIMER. Risky! Very risky! No place to bring a white woman.
ALICE. But why not?
SIR MORTIMER. Can't trust the natives. Shifty lot. Never look you in the eye.

ALICE. But girls go simply everywhere these days.
SIR MORTIMER. Not up the Beanstalk. Beanstalk. Beanstalk! Did somebody really mention Beanstalk?
JACK (*indicating it*) Of course! Look!
SIR MORTIMER. Begad, there it is! Well I'll be—hrmm! So they've reopened the Beanstalk Line!
JACK. And a good job, too. We're just in time to save your Excellency from a dastardly plot.
SIR MORTIMER. What, another? Those Croakers again, I suppose?
JACK. The butler and the housekeeper.
SIR MORTIMER (*picking up the tea-cup*) As I thought! Well, now, suppose you tell me all about it while I have me tea. Eh?

(ALICE *snatches his cup and empties it through the window*)

Here, what the . . . ? My Earl Grey!
JACK. It's Mandragora's Drowsy Syrup. Part of the plot!
SIR MORTIMER (*sniffing the teapot*) Poison, begad! Well, let this be a warning to you. Take a tip from an old campaigner and Never Trust the Natives!

No. 10 SONG: NEVER TRUST THE NATIVES (SIR MORTIMER, JACK *and* ALICE)

(*During the chorus they march round in Indian file, peering warily under their palms as though following a jungle track with hostile natives in the undergrowth*)

SIR MORTIMER.
    Never trust the natives when you come to Fairyland,
    They talk a funny lingo that you cannot understand;
    Miss Enid Blyton told me and it's absolutely true
    You may believe in fairies but they won't believe in you.
ALL.
    O never trust the natives, they are sinister and sly,
    So understand, in Fairyland you must keep your powder dry,
    Your rifle at the ready, it's the only thing to do,
    But never trust the natives for they don't trust you!
SIR MORTIMER.
    Never trust the natives, for the fairies and the elves
    Are both inclined, as you will find, to get above themselves;
    They treat you like a foreigner, which really is a bore
    When anyone can see that you are British to the core.
ALL. O never trust the natives, etc.
SIR MORTIMER.
    The waiters are impertinent, the taxi-men are fools,
    The leaders of the nation haven't been to public schools;

The sanitation's primitive, the cooking a disgrace,
So take my tip and never trust the natives of the place.
ALL. O never trust the natives, etc.
SIR MORTIMER.
Never trust the natives, for their tastes are very queer;
They'd rather drink their cowslip wine than honest British
   beer,
You can't get eggs and bacon or a decent cup of tea,
And fifty years of Fairyland is quite enough for me.
ALL. O never trust the natives, or they'll stab you in the back!
Just look behind, you're sure to find a fairy on your track:
The bones of better men than you are littered everywhere,
So when you come to Fairyland beware, beware!

JACK. I must say this is all quite a surprise. I'd no idea that Fairyland was so undeveloped.
SIR MORTIMER. Backward country, very backward. Go a day's march without seeing a single hansom cab.
ALICE. I say, you have been away a long time.
SIR MORTIMER. Best years of me life.
JACK. Then why not resign and come home with us?
SIR MORTIMER. Nothing I'd like better, if it wasn't for the P.M.
ALICE. Who's the P.M.?
JACK. He means the Prime Minister.
SIR MORTIMER. Quite right, young feller. "Me boy," says the P.M., "there's just one place I'd like to see you in, and that place is Fairyland." And he meant it.
JACK. I'm sure he did. And what did you say?
SIR MORTIMER. "Thank you, Mr Disraeli."
JACK. Mr Disraeli? But he isn't Prime Minister any more.
SIR MORTIMER. What? Don't tell me that bounder Gladstone's in again!
JACK. Never mind politics. What are we going to do about the Croakers? They'll be here at any moment.
ALICE (*at the door*) I believe I hear them now.
JACK (*saluting*) Sir, patrol reports enemy activity.
SIR MORTIMER. Action stations! Patrol, 'shun!

(JACK *and* ALICE *spring to attention.* SIR MORTIMER *produces a toy gun, water pistol and telescope. He keeps the gun, gives the water pistol to Jack and the telescope to Alice*)

Slope arms! Steady the Buffs!

(*The Hen cackles*)

And the Buff Orpingtons! (*He moves the table down* R) Platoon, retire to prepared positions!

(JACK *and* ALICE *make a barricade with the table and chair.* SIR MORTIMER *dons a pith helmet and sticks a small Union Jack on the barricade. They all crouch behind the barricade, pointing their weapons at the door*)

Rifles at the ready, and don't shoot until you can see the whites of their eyes!
ALICE. But I can't shoot with a telescope.
SIR MORTIMER. No, but you can see the whites of their eyes.
JACK. But this is only a water pistol!
SIR MORTIMER. As issued to the Home Guard.

(*He sings,* JACK *and* ALICE *joining in*)
ALL. The Croakers are coming, oh ho, oh ho!
The Croakers are coming, oh ho, oh ho!
The Croakers are coming to capture the castle
But they'll be unlucky, oh ho, oh ho!

(CROAKER *enters* L, *followed by* MRS CROAKER. CROAKER *wears a bowler and carries a Gladstone bag and umbrella.* MRS CROAKER *wears a bonnet and carries a bulging shopping-bag*)

SIR MORTIMER. Halt! Who goes there?
CROAKER. Only me, sir. That is, me and my good lady.

(MRS CROAKER *curtsies*)

SIR MORTIMER. And where d'you think you're going?
CROAKER. To Blackpool.
SIR MORTIMER. With my treasure and my magic hen? Eh? Come on, man, speak up!
CROAKER. That was the idea.
SIR MORTIMER. Archibald Croaker, you're a confounded blackguard!
CROAKER }
MRS CROAKER } (*reproachfully*) Sir!
SIR MORTIMER. You, too, ma'am!
MRS CROAKER. I'm sure we've done our best to give satisfaction.
SIR MORTIMER. Satisfaction? You and your dragon dumplings! Ugh!

(MRS CROAKER *weeps.* CROAKER *comforts her*)

CROAKER. Now look what you've done. There, there, he didn't mean it.
SIR MORTIMER. Stop snivelling, ma'am, and attend to me. Archibald and Ermyntrude Croaker.
CROAKER }
MRS CROAKER } Sir?
SIR MORTIMER. Do you surrender to the forces of law and order?

ACT II STORY OF JACK AND THE BEANSTALK

CROAKER. Sorry, nothing doing. Will there be anything more, sir?

(MRS CROAKER *approaches the Hen. It cackles*)

SIR MORTIMER. Leave that bird alone!
CROAKER. Carry on, Ermyntrude.
SIR MORTIMER. Mutiny, begad! Platoon, charge!

(SIR MORTIMER, JACK *and* ALICE *close with the* CROAKERS. CROAKER *trips* JACK *and attacks* SIR MORTIMER *with his umbrella.* MRS CROAKER *overpowers* ALICE. JACK *gets up*)

JACK. I know! The Drowsy Syrup!

(*He fills his water pistol from the teapot and squirts it at the* CROAKERS. *They reel, stagger and collapse.* SIR MORTIMER *grabs the umbrella and whacks Croaker with it*)

CROAKER (*dreamily*) Ermyntrude, my dear, I can see the Blackpool illuminations.
MRS CROAKER. Can you? I can't.

(SIR MORTIMER *whacks her with the umbrella*)

Oh yes, there they are. Lovely!
SIR MORTIMER. Victory! Well done, young feller, I'll see you're mentioned in despatches.
JACK (*saluting*) Thank you, sir.
SIR MORTIMER. How many prisoners?
JACK (*counting*) Two, sir.
SIR MORTIMER. Two, eh? Dead or alive?
CROAKER. Dead.
SIR MORTIMER. Wasn't asking you. Sergeant?
JACK. Sir, I think they're alive.
SIR MORTIMER. You do, eh? Well, in any case you'd better take 'em to the guard-room under armed escort.
JACK. The guard-room? Where's that?
SIR MORTIMER. The castle dungeon—this way.

(ALICE *stirs up the* CROAKERS *with the wand*)

JACK. Prisoners, attention! Come on, jump to it.

(*The* CROAKERS *get up*)

JACK. Right turn, quick march!
SIR MORTIMER. To the dungeon! And remember—Never Trust the Natives!

REPRISE of No. 10

(SIR MORTIMER *leads* JACK, ALICE *and the* CROAKERS *out* L. *The* 1ST FAIRY *enters cautiously* R)

1st Fairy.
Now where's that wand of mine? I feel quite sure
I left it lying somewhere on the floor.
What shall I do if it's been stolen by
The Wicked Giant or a Foreign spy?

(*She continues the search. The strain of "Never Trust the Natives" is heard as* Jack, Alice *and* Sir Mortimer *return*)

But hark—an awe-inspiring martial strain!
The Beanstalk Expedition once again.
I'd better hide in here, or I shall be
Caught by the bold licentious soldieree.

(*The* 1st Fairy *hides in a fold of the curtain.*
Jack, Alice *and* Sir Mortimer *return*)

Sir Mortimer. Well, that's taken care of the prisoners. Much obliged to you, me boy—and you, too, me dear.
Jack. It's a pleasure, your Excellency.
Sir Mortimer. And now, what about a spot of tiffin, eh?
Jack. It's very kind of you, sir. But I really think we ought to be getting back to Mangel-Wurzel-on-the-Wold.
Sir Mortimer. Mangel-Wurzel? You don't mean to tell me you come from dear old Mangel-Wurzel?
Jack. Mangel-Wurzel born and bred.
Sir Mortimer. Well, I'll be . . . ! Come here, me boy, and let's have a look at you. Begad, if you aren't the living image of Molly Madcap.
Jack. Molly Madcap? But that was my mother's maiden name?
Sir Mortimer. Me boy, shake hands with the man who might have been your father.
Jack. Why, then you must be . . .
Alice. The Old Squire! Sir Mortimer Mortiboy!
Sir Mortimer. Your servant, ma'am.
Jack. Wait till mother hears about this!
Sir Mortimer. And how is me old flame these days? Still a fine figure of a woman, I'll be bound!
Jack. Very fine—for a widow.
Sir Mortimer. A widow, eh? D'you know, after what you've told me I've a good mind to chuck this job and settle down in dear old Mangel-Wurzel.
Jack. Why don't you? I'm sure everybody would be glad to have you back.
Sir Mortimer. Would they, begad! After all, why shouldn't I? Me diplomatic mission's accomplished.
Jack. What exactly *was* your diplomatic mission?
Sir Mortimer. Mustn't ask. State secret.
Alice. Was it very secret?

Act II STORY OF JACK AND THE BEANSTALK

SIR MORTIMER. Me dear, it's so dashed secret they wouldn't even tell *me*.
JACK. But surely you knew what you were doing?
SIR MORTIMER. Me boy, how little you know about the Foreign Office.
JACK. Anyway, I'm sure it's high time you rested on your well-earned laurels.
SIR MORTIMER. And so I will, begad! Let's fetch the iron rations from the cook-house—and off we'll all go to Mangel-Wurzel and Molly Madcap!

(SIR MORTIMER, JACK *and* ALICE *exit* L, *singing* "*Never Trust the Natives*". *The* 1ST FAIRY *comes down* C)

1ST FAIRY. I see—their fell design to journey hence is
With secret plans of Fairyland defences:
But I know how to stop their little game,
And send them home much quicker than they came.

(*He blows a whistle*)

By fairy troops the castle is surrounded,
Ablaze with patriotic zeal unbounded.

(*Armed* FAIRIES *appear at the window*)

My friends, our enemies are in our power—
At least, they will be in—say half-an-hour:
They plan to travel by the Beanstalk line;
So to your places, there await the sign;
And know, when I do sound my warning blast
(*He blows the whistle*)
Our cunning foes, like sailors to a mast
Do cling to soaring beanstalk branches dizzy:
O, then must you with saw and axe get busy,
Till Beanstalk, Giant, boy and girl and all,
Down, down to well-deserved death do fall!
Are my instructions clear?

2ND FAIRY.   As clear as day!
1ST FAIRY. Then each one to his post. Dispatch, away!

(*The* 1ST FAIRY *retires behind the curtain. The other* FAIRIES *exit.*
JACK, ALICE *and* SIR MORTIMER *return* L)

ALICE. Thank goodness, the Beanstalk's still there.
JACK. I should hope so.
ALICE. I have an awful feeling it may vanish at any moment.
SIR MORTIMER. Then all aboard—get your landing tickets from the purser. Wait! Just take a look at me, young feller. Now, would you say this was the right kit for Beanstalk climbing?
JACK. Well—I don't think Sir Edmund Hillary would approve.

SIR MORTIMER. How right you are! (*He takes off the dressing-gown and comes down* C) Where's me fancy wesket? Me frock coat? Look alive, there, give a hand.

(JACK *and* ALICE *help him to complete his toilet. They dash about with various garments*)

ALICE. Do hurry, please!

SIR MORTIMER. Me topper—me button-hole—me silk handkerchief! Me cane—me gloves—me dispatch-case! Brush and shine! That's the ticket—all ready for kit inspection!

(*He is at last the complete diplomat. They pick up the Hen and the bags, etc.*)

JACK (*jumping on to the Beanstalk*) Thank goodness! Come on, Sir Mortimer—it's quite safe!

SIR MORTIMER. Is it, begad! (*To Alice*) After you, me dear.

ALICE. Oh no, after you.

JACK. Make up your minds or we'll be all day.

SIR MORTIMER. Sure you wouldn't feel safer if we were all roped together?

ALICE. *I* wouldn't.

SIR MORTIMER. Oh! Very well, then. Floreat Etona! Mortiboy omnia vincit!

(SIR MORTIMER *and* ALICE *prepare to join Jack on the Beanstalk. The* 1ST FAIRY *comes down raising his whistle to his lips*)

1ST FAIRY. Now Beanstalk, break! and Mortiboy, descend
Through empty air to thine appointed end!

(*The* CROAKERS *enter* L. CROAKER *carries a blunderbuss*)

CROAKER. Please elevate your hands above your head.

1ST FAIRY. Help, help! A spectre rising from the dead!

(*The* 1ST FAIRY *runs off, dropping his whistle. The* CROAKERS *advance* R)

SIR MORTIMER. The Croakers, begad!

JACK. But we locked them in the dungeon!

CROAKER. The locks were rusty and the fetters rotten.

MRS CROAKER. The brittle bolts and bars we broke like cotton.

SIR MORTIMER. Look here, I told you to consider yourselves under arrest.

CROAKER. And so we did—but now, with your permission
It's time to reconsider our position.
Accept defeat, madam and gentlemen;
Throw down your treasure and the magic hen.

SIR MORTIMER. Begad!

ACT II STORY OF JACK AND THE BEANSTALK 41

ALICE. What shall we do?
JACK. Our only course is
To strike our flag before superior forces.

(*They drop the Hen, bags, etc., and move down*)

But never mind—we soon will find a way
To turn the tables and to win the day.
CROAKER. Come, Ermyntrude, and gather up the swag!
SIR MORTIMER. Confound her, that's the diplomatic bag!
MRS CROAKER. Ungenerous Giant, this we take in lieu
Of wages many quarters overdue.

(*The* CROAKERS *mount the Beanstalk with the Hen, bags, etc.*)

CROAKER. And now to Mangel-Wurzel with the loot
By this the cheapest and the quickest route.
MRS CROAKER. But first, lest these our foes should follow us,
Put them to silence with your blunderbuss.

(CROAKER *takes aim with the blunderbuss.* JACK *and* ALICE *cling together.* SIR MORTIMER *sees the whistle and picks it up*)

JACK. At least spare Alice!
CROAKER. Useless now to whine!
SIR MORTIMER. Help! Murder! Police! (*He blows the whistle*)
Dial nine-nine-nine!
MRS CROAKER. Quick, pull the trigger!

(*The Beanstalk sways.* CROAKER *drops the blunderbuss and grabs Mrs Croaker*)

JACK. Look, the Beanstalk's shaking!
CROAKER. Jump, Ermyntrude!
JACK. Too late—the Beanstalk's breaking!

(*The* CROAKERS, *struggling, sink out of sight. The others rush to the window. The* FAIRIES *cheer below*)

SIR MORTIMER. Begad! Those dashed fairies have cut the Beanstalk Line!
JACK. At least they'll be home before we shall.
SIR MORTIMER. Question is, how do we get to Mangel-Wurzel now?
JACK. How did you get here in the first place?
SIR MORTIMER. Chartered a Victorian Airways balloon. Wouldn't care to risk it a second time, though. Don't trust these modern contraptions.

42   STORY OF JACK AND THE BEANSTALK   Act II

ALICE. Perhaps the fairies will help us. After all they saved us from the Croakers.

SIR MORTIMER. So they did, begad!

JACK. But only by accident. The Croakers fell into a trap meant for us.

SIR MORTIMER. There you are! What did I tell you? Never can trust the natives.

(*The* 1ST FAIRY *enters, attended by armed* FAIRIES)

1ST FAIRY. What, mortals, still alive? Fairies, secure 'em,
And in the dungeon desolate immure 'em.
Fling down your arms—I call on you to yield.

JACK (*seizing the wand*)
Not while I still have strength this wand to wield!

(JACK, *with the wand, and* SIR MORTIMER, *with his cane, fight the* FAIRIES, *but are overpowered*)

1ST FAIRY. Your cause is lost—all further struggle's vain.

ALICE (*at the window*)
I say, the Beanstalk's growing once again!

SIR MORTIMER. Why, so it is, begad!

1ST FAIRY.   Look out, be wary!
It is a trick!

(*The Beanstalk reappears at the window with the* BEANSTALK FAIRY, *crowned*)

ALICE.   Hooray, the Beanstalk Fairy!

BEANSTALK FAIRY.
What ho within there! Peace, I charge you, peace!
Upon the instant let this clamour cease!
How dare you thus receive these mortals brave
They are my friends.

1ST FAIRY.   Your majesty, we crave
Your royal pardon.

JACK.   Why, what does this mean?

BEANSTALK FAIRY.
Can you not guess? I am the Fairy Queen.

ALICE. The Fairy Queen! I'd always longed to see her,
Although I'd never dreamed that you could be her.

BEANSTALK FAIRY.
This gentleman I'm sure I've met before.

SIR MORTIMER. Mortiboy, ma'am—the Diplomatic Corps.

Act II STORY OF JACK AND THE BEANSTALK

(*The* BEANSTALK FAIRY *comes down into the room.* ALICE *curtsies, the others bow. The* BEANSTALK FAIRY *assumes a European social manner, extending her hand to* SIR MORTIMER *to kiss*)

BEANSTALK FAIRY. Ah, Sir Mortimer, of course! How are you, and what has your Government been up to lately?
SIR MORTIMER (*feeling in his pocket and producing a crumpled paper*) Where's me last dispatch? Ah, here we are! I am happy to inform your Majesty that Mafeking has been relieved.
BEANSTALK FAIRY. And so have you, Sir Mortimer.
SIR MORTIMER. Eh, ma'am? What's that?
BEANSTALK FAIRY. Your Government has relieved you of your ambassadorial post. As from tomorrow you are appointed second secretary to the British Embassy in Hampstead.*
SIR MORTIMER. Begad! Promotion at last!
BEANSTALK FAIRY. My congratulations. No-one knows better than I how well you have deserved this honour.
SIR MORTIMER. Ma'am, you overwhelm me.
BEANSTALK FAIRY. Anglo-Fairy relations have never been better—thanks to your masterly inactivity. Allow me to invest you with the Most Excellent Order of Titania—a donkey rampant on a green field.

(*She decorates him.* ALL *cheer*)

SIR MORTIMER. Much obliged, ma'am. And now—I hate to mention this, but could you possibly lend me a fiver till pay day?
BEANSTALK FAIRY. But Sir Mortimer, I understood you were a wealthy man.
SIR MORTIMER. So I was, ma'am, until those dashed Croakers cleaned me out.

(FAIRIES *enter leading the* CROAKERS, *bound. Some* FAIRIES *are carrying the Croakers' bags and the Magic Hen*)

JACK. Why, here they are!
SIR MORTIMER. Me treasure! Me magic hen!
BEANSTALK FAIRY.
    Their passport photos they did not resemble:
    Unhappy couple, hear my wrath and tremble!
    Go, stew your teas in those funereal urns
    To which no traveller of sense returns;
    Be ye condemned forever to the gloom
    Of Fairy Railways grim Refreshment Room!
SIR MORTIMER. And serve 'em right!
CROAKER. ⎱   What base ingratitude
MRS CROAKER. ⎰ To faithful Archibald and Ermyntrude!
BEANSTALK FAIRY. Come, gentle Jack and Alice, kiss my hand—

---

* Or some other familiar and improbable place.

	It's time to bid farewell to Fairyland.
JACK.	Farewell, dear Beanstalk Fairy—I should say Your Majesty. Perhaps another day We'll meet again?
BEANSTALK FAIRY.	Aye, very probablee; At least, I hope so, Jack.
ALICE.	And so do we.
SIR MORTIMER.	Come on, me boy—the Beanstalk's waiting for us: Salute the Fairies with a final chorus.

(*They mount the Beanstalk*)

No. 10a *Repeat of No. 5a* CHORUS (SIR MORTIMER, JACK *and* ALICE)

    Good-bye, Fairies!
    Good-bye, Fairies!
    Good-bye, Fairies!
    We're bound to leave you now,
    Down the Beanstalk, down we go!
    Down we go,
    Down we go!
    Down the Beanstalk, down we go,
    We'll be home for tea.

(*Quick* CURTAIN *rising on tableau*—JACK, ALICE *and* SIR MORTIMER *have disappeared down the Beanstalk and the* FAIRIES *are waving to them from the window*)

CURTAIN

ACT III

Scene—*The Village Green.*

It is the same as Act I, except that the roofs, etc. have been repaired, the houses have TV aerials and there is a general air of prosperity. The "To Let" and "For Sale" signs have disappeared. One cottage has become "Beanstalk View Private Hotel". The butcher's shop is advertising "Salmon Teas" and in the window of "The Flying Horse" is a "House Full" notice.

From the middle of the village green rises the Beanstalk. To it are attached ribbons for use in the Maypole Dance.

When the Curtain *rises,* Jack *is helping* Alice *down from the Beanstalk. Lighting should suggest an early summer morning.*

Jack.	Well, here we are, my dear—all danger past, In Mangel-Wurzel safely home at last.
Alice.	But where's the Squire?
Jack.	We passed him long ago: He'll catch us up in half an hour or so.
Alice.	How strange I feel! As though we'd been away Six months at least instead of just a day.
Jack.	And so do I. I just don't understand— Alice, what time did we leave Fairyland?
Alice.	At three upon a winter afternoon.
Jack.	But surely we return to radiant June, And eastward, look, the morning sun is bright!
Alice.	And dear old Mangel-Wurzel's altered quite; It has an air of new prosperitee— Why, all the cottages have got TV!

(Simon *comes out of the shop and gapes*)

Jack.	'The Flying Horse' is full!
Alice.	And, if you please, Father is advertising Salmon Teas!
Simon.	It's Alice and Jack! Alice and Jack! Safe and sound— Well, I'll be bound!

(*He embraces them.*
Mrs Durden *enters from "The Flying Horse"*)

MRS DURDEN. It's Jack, it's Jack!
My boy has come back!
I'm quite at a loss—
I ought to be cross,
But I'm too overjoyed
To pretend I'm annoyed!

(MRS DURDEN *weeps. She and* JACK *embrace.* SIMON *and* ALICE *embrace.*
GRIMSHANK *comes out of his shop*)

GRIMSHANK. Now, what's all this 'ere?
Eh, Alice me dear,
Come back to your Dad?
I'm ever so glad!

(*More embraces.*
GAFFER DRIBBLEDRIP *enters* L, *wearing a peaked cap and ticket-punch*)

GAFFER. Eh, what a to-do!
'Ello, it's them two!
I'll be blowed, they've come back!
Alice and Jack—
If I were their father I'd give 'em a smack! (*He sits on the bench*)

MRS DURDEN. You naughty children, we've been so worried. Six months and never a picture postcard.
JACK. Six months? Have we really been away as long as that?
MRS DURDEN. You know very well you have.
ALICE. So fairy time *is* different.
GRIMSHANK. Fairy time? You'll be telling us next you've been to Fairyland.
JACK. And so we have.
SIMON. Oo, what a fib! (*He crosses and talks to* GAFFER)
ALICE. It isn't a fib! We climbed up the Beanstalk . . .
MRS DURDEN. Goodness gracious!
GRIMSHANK. Up the Beanstalk? But you couldn't have!
JACK. But we did! And who do you think we found?
GRIMSHANK. Burgess and Maclean?*
JACK. No. The Old Squire!
MRS DURDEN. Morty? You found my Morty? Is he married?
JACK. Still a susceptible bachelor!
MRS DURDEN. Thank goodness!
ALICE. And in less than half an hour Sir Mortimer will be here.
MRS DURDEN. Here? Morty? He's coming back to me after all these years! My Morty!

* Or other prominent missing persons.

Act III STORY OF JACK AND THE BEANSTALK 47

(*She weeps. They pat her on the back, etc.*)

GAFFER. Eh? Wot were that?
SIMON. They found the Old Squire.
GAFFER. 'Oo?
SIMON. Old Squire!
GAFFER. 'Ere, 'oo are you callin' an Owd Liar?

(*They argue for a few moments, then* SIMON *fetches two beer-mugs from* "*The Flying Horse*")

GRIMSHANK. If I was you I'd be ashamed, that's what I'd be. Leading a poor old woman up the garden path.
MRS DURDEN. Old woman yourself!
ALICE. But, Father, it's true—every word!
GRIMSHANK. A girl who tells lies is no daughter of mine.
ALICE. But, Father . . .
GRIMSHANK. Tell the truth or never darken my doors no more.
ALICE. But it *is* the truth!
GRIMSHANK. Then 'enceforth you 'ave neither 'ome nor father.

(GRIMSHANK *goes into his shop and slams the door*)

ALICE. What shall I do now?
MRS DURDEN. Never mind him, dear. Let's all go and meet Morty's train.
JACK. But, Mother, he isn't coming by train.
MRS DURDEN. Then how is he coming?
JACK. Down the Beanstalk.
MRS DURDEN. Down the Beanstalk? At his age? Oh, you cruel children! Expecting me to believe a tale like that!
JACK. Mother, please listen . . .
MRS DURDEN. That's enough now. I must go and look after the lodgers—I mean the guests. Oh, business is booming!

(*She goes towards* "*The Flying Horse*". JACK *and* ALICE *follow*)

And where do you think you're going? Can't you read?
JACK. "House Full"? But surely that doesn't apply to me?
MRS DURDEN. It certainly does. I've let your room to the guest of honour.
JACK. And who's he?
MRS DURDEN. The gentleman from the BBC.

(MRS DURDEN *goes into* "*The Flying Horse*" *and slams the door*)

ALICE. Oh dear, nobody wants us. Whatever shall we do?
JACK. I know, let's get engaged and then we can put our names down for a council house.
GAFFER. Now then, you two. Got yer tickets?
JACK. Tickets? What for?
GAFFER. To see the Beanstalk. Bob a nob.

JACK. Well, I like that! Why should *we* pay to see the Beanstalk? They ought to pay us for climbing it.
GAFFER. Wot were that?
SIMON. Say they've climbed up Beanstalk.
GAFFER. Up Beanstalk? Wot? Them two?
SIMON. So they say.

(SIMON *and* GAFFER *point at Jack and Alice and burst out laughing.* SIMON *goes into the shop,* GAFFER *into "The Flying Horse"*)

ALICE. Really, it's too bad. Won't anybody believe us?
JACK. I know someone who will. Come on, let's go and find her.
ALICE. Whoever do you mean?
JACK. Our only friend in all Mangel-Wurzel—dear old Maisie Moo-cow.

No. 11 BALLAD (JACK)

JACK. Returning to reception cold
    We don't know what to do;
The tale of Jack and Sherpa bold
Says Mangel-Wurzel-on-the-Wold
    Is a tale untrue.
I think it's just too bad—don't you?
Hard lines on local lad—and you!
    Our only friend
    At journey's end
A little cow that says, "Moo, moo!"

(JACK *and* ALICE *exit* R.

The VILLAGE CHILDREN *enter and move down* C, *dancing and singing*)

No. 12 CHORUS (VILLAGE CHILDREN)

CHILDREN. Come, lasses and lads,
    Get leave of your dads,
And away to the Beanstalk hie;
    Rehearsal call
    For one and all—
The producer's standing by;
    For we've a date, you see,
    With sponsored Tele—V—
The Beany, Beany, Beany, Beany,
    Beany Kids are we:
The Beany, Beany, Beany, Beany,
    Beany Kids are we.

(*As the Chorus ends,* BLENKINSOP *of the BBC comes out of "The Flying Horse" rubbing his hands*)

Act III STORY OF JACK AND THE BEANSTALK

BLENKINSOP. Good morning, Beanies!
CHILDREN. Good morning, Mr Blenkinsop.
BLENKINSOP. And how are we all this lovely morning? On top of the world? Bursting with buck and Beanies?
CHILDREN. Yes, thank you, Mr Blenkinsop.
BLENKINSOP. And just why do we feel so good? Now, who can tell me?

(A CHILD *raises her hand*)

Ah, there's a clever little girl! Well, dear?
1ST CHILD. Because there's no school today.
BLENKINSOP. We'll have to do better than that or we'll never be a Queen Beany. No! We're all feeling fit because we've had heaped-up platefuls of crisp crunchy Beanies for breakfast. Haven't we?
CHILDREN. NO!
BLENKINSOP. Oh? Well, don't tell the televiewers or your contract's cancelled. And remember—the way to succeed in commercial radio is to start as I did—at the bottom of the ladder.
1ST CHILD. And where's that?
BLENKINSOP. Broadcasting House. Listen and I'll tell you the inspiring story of my career.

(SIMON *and* GRIMSHANK *come out of the shop,* GAFFER *and* MRS DURDEN *out of "The Flying Horse"*)

No. 13 SONG (BLENKINSOP *and* CHORUS)

BLENKINSOP.   When I was a lad I thought I'd earn
              An honest copper as a comic turn.
              I played in pantomime as Idle Jack,
              I wasn't very funny and I'd just one crack,
                  But I cracked that crack so constantlee
                  That I soon became a comic on the BBC!
CHORUS.   But he cracked that crack so constantlee
                  That he soon became a comic on the BBC!
BLENKINSOP.   As an actor then I thought I'd star,
              But oh how difficult producers are!
              They took one look at my mobile face,
              And promptly packed me off again to Portland
                  Place.
                  Not a weekly rep. had a part for me,
                  So I imitated seagulls for the BBC!
CHORUS.   And nobody's quite as good as he
                  At imitating seagulls for the BBC!
BLENKINSOP.   But my brow grew higher and I wooed the art
              Of profound Beethoven and sublime Mozart.

BLENKINSOP. I can't tell a quaver from a semitone,
   But I'm quite a virtuoso on the gramophone.
   Yes, I played my records so brilliantlee
   I became a Family Favourite on the BBC!
CHORUS. Yes, he played, etc.
BLENKINSOP. A commentator I then became,
   But I still inspired to a nobler fame.
   At last I've realized my boyhood dream—
   A member of the Twenty Questions Team!
   And Gilbert's jealous of my repartee,
   Which makes him nasty-tempered on the BBC!
CHORUS. Yes, Gilbert's jealous, etc.
BLENKINSOP. Now Broadcasting House has had its day,
   But commercial television's here to stay,
   And on Monday nights we'll meet, I hope,
   By courtesy of Supalatha Shaving Soap—
   Yes, they've signed me up at a higher salaree
   Than the dear Director-General of the BBC!
CHORUS. Yes, they've signed him up, etc.

(*The* BEANSTALK FAIRY *enters*)

BLENKINSOP. Thank you, Beanies. And now we'll have a straight run-through of the maypole dance round the Beany Beanstalk. Positions, please. (*To the Beanstalk Fairy*) Excuse me, madam, no visitors allowed here today.

BEANSTALK FAIRY.
   No visitors? What nonsense, I declare!
   The village green's a public thoroughfare.

BLENKINSOP. Not today it isn't. Ask Beany Breakfast Foods Limited. They've hired it—Beanstalk and all.

BEANSTALK FAIRY.
   Young man, I am disgusted and surprised
   To find my Beanstalk thus commercialized.

GRIMSHANK.
   That Beanstalk, ma'am, if I may make so bold,
   Belongs to Mangel-Wurzel-on-the-Wold,
   By whose consent that smart young fellow here is
   To film it for his television series.

BEANSTALK FAIRY.
   You've cashed in on the picture postcard racket;
   By Dainty Teas you've made a pretty packet;
   There's not an empty bed in that hotel—
   Why, Mangel-Wurzel's never done so well!

Act III   STORY OF JACK AND THE BEANSTALK   51

Mrs Durden.
  Assuming that the things you say are true,
  I don't see what they've got to do with you.
Beanstalk Fairy.
  Let me inform you, ma'am, the Beanstalk's mine—
  At Beany Breakfast Foods I draw the line!
Gaffer. You've seen the Beanstalk, mum?
Beanstalk Fairy.   Of course I've seen it!
Gaffer. Then that'll be a bob.
Beanstalk Fairy.   You cannot mean it!
  This is outrageous! Can't I even see
  My own Beanstalk unless I pay a fee?
Gaffer. A bob a nob!
Grimshank.   He's right—that's Council rule—
  Half-price to pensioners and kids at school.
Blenkinsop.
  May I point out we pay ten quid a minute
  To make this film—I'm waiting to begin it.
Beanstalk Fairy.
  I'll bandy words no longer! Carry on!
  Be sure of this—you'll hear from me anon!

(*The* Beanstalk Fairy *exits*)

Blenkinsop. What a dreadful woman! Mr Mayor, I do hope we shan't have any more interruptions.

Grimshank. Not if I can 'elp it.

Blenkinsop. Very well. Carry on, Beanies—one straight run-through then we'll shoot.

(Blenkinsop *exits. There is a maypole dance round the Beanstalk. As it draws to a close* Blenkinsop's *voice is heard over a loudspeaker*)

Blenkinsop. Have you a beanstalk in your back garden? You haven't? Never mind—take a tip from the Beany Kids and keep a packet of crisp crunchy Beanies on your breakfast-table. Remember, it's the ten-second Beany breakfast that fills you just as full of beans as the famous Mangel-Wurzel Beanstalk. And be sure to join the Beany Kids next week in another jolly game with Uncle Bill Blenkinsop.

(Blenkinsop *reappears carrying a microphone and a cine-camera*)

Yes, I know it's lousy but that's the way they want it.

(Jack *and* Alice *enter with* Maisie. Maisie *joins the maypole dance.* Blenkinsop *chases Maisie and gets tangled with ribbons*)

Here, what's this—a fiesta? Cut it, you kids. Cut it, I tell you or the deal's off!

(*The dance ends. The* CHILDREN *unravel* BLENKINSOP)

Come on, come on, let's get it in the can! At any rate it can't be worse than last time.

(*The dance starts again.* BLENKINSOP *operates his cine-camera. The* BEANSTALK FAIRY *enters*)

O.K., shoot!

BEANSTALK FAIRY.
    Beany children, cease your tripping!
    Terminate your sponsored skipping!
    Magic Beanstalk, hence away,
    Fairy Majesty obey!
    Fly to some enchanted Arden,
    Haunted grove or palace garden!

(*The Beanstalk rises and vanishes. Everyone reacts.*)

JACK.   The Beanstalk Fairy!
MRS DURDEN (*jumping*)   Help me catch it, quick!
BLENKINSOP. This is the end!
GRIMSHANK.   Eh, what a dirty trick!
JACK.   But where's Sir Mortimer?
ALICE.   He hasn't landed!
BEANSTALK FAIRY.
    I quite forgot! In mid-air he'll be stranded!

(*Sir Mortimer's top-hat falls from above*)

JACK.   Do something quickly, please!
ALICE.   Hello, what's that?
JACK (*picking up the hat*)
    Goodness, the poor old gentleman's top-hat!
    He can't be far away!
BEANSTALK FAIRY.   I go to meet him
    Rely on me, and very soon you'll greet him!

(*The* BEANSTALK FAIRY *disappears*)

GAFFER (*pointing up into the auditorium*) Look! One o' them there aerobatics!
JACK. Why, it's Sir Mortimer on a parachute! Hooray, he's baled out of the Beanstalk.
GAFFER. Lad's right! If it bain't Owd Squire!

(*All come down and point to indicate the downward wafting of Sir Mortimer*)

MRS DURDEN (*waving*) Morty! Morty! It's Molly!

(*A drum-crash indicates Sir Mortimer's arrival*)

JACK. Hooray, he's landed!
GAFFER. Three cheers for t'Owd Squire! 'Ip, 'ip . . .

(*Cheers as* SIR MORTIMER *enters trailing a small parachute and carrying the Hen and baggage.* JACK *gives him his top-hat.* JACK *and* ALICE *take the bags and the Hen.* BLENKINSOP *brings the microphone down*)

GRIMSHANK. Welcome, sir—welcome back to Mangel-Wurzel.
SIR MORTIMER (*extending his arms*) England, Home . . .
MRS DURDEN. And Beauty!
SIR MORTIMER. Beauty, begad! (*He kisses the village girls*) Dashed if I can remember which of you is little Molly Madcap!
MRS DURDEN (*tapping him on the back*) Oh, you naughty boy, Mortiboy!
SIR MORTIMER (*turning*) You have the advantage of me, ma'am.
MRS DURDEN. Morty! Surely you haven't forgotten me?
SIR MORTIMER (*recognizing her*) Begad! Molly, me old sport! Come and give me a smacker!

(MRS DURDEN *gives him a "smacker"*)

MRS DURDEN. I may have lost my girlish bloom . . .
JACK. But she's still a fine figure of a woman.
SIR MORTIMER. So she is, begad! And in me mind's eye she's the same frisky little filly I knew in the old days.
MRS DURDEN. Go along with you, Morty!
SIR MORTIMER. In me mind's eye. Must remember to keep the other eye closed. Jack, me lad.
JACK. Sir?
SIR MORTIMER. Pop over to Mortiboy Hall, there's a good chap, and tell Merriman to send the horse and gig.

(*He chats to* ALICE)

JACK (*puzzled; to Mrs Durden*) Merriman?
MRS DURDEN. The old butler—dead these forty years.
SIR MORTIMER (*to Jack*) Tell him we'll be dining at seven.
JACK (*aside*) Poor Sir Mortimer! How can we ever tell him that Mortiboy Hall's a rest home for civil servants?
SIR MORTIMER (*to Mrs Durden*) Tell you what, me dear. After dinner we'll drink bubbly out of your slipper and have a bonfire on the terrace. (*To Jack*) Hey, young feller—thought I told you to fetch the gig?

(JACK *looks at Mrs Durden*)

MRS DURDEN. It isn't his fault, Morty. You see—well, Mr Merriman isn't with us any more.

Sir Mortimer. Eh? You don't mean . . . ? Poor Merriman! Cut off in his prime!
Mrs Durden. He *was* eighty-seven.
Sir Mortimer (*firmly*) In his prime. (*To Jack*) Well, then, fetch young Parker.

(Mrs Durden *shakes her head at Jack*)

Jack. I'm sorry, sir, but . . .
Sir Mortimer. What? Parker, too? Begad! Don't tell me Parker's dead!
Mrs Durden. He isn't dead—he's in the House of Commons.
Sir Mortimer. Begad! (*He takes off hat and bows his head*)
Mrs Durden. There now, Morty. It's been a long time, you know.
Sir Mortimer. Yes, yes. Too long. But—surely there must be *someone*? If only I could remember . . . (*Suddenly he brightens*) Wait! The pantry boy—queer name—got it! Young Tom Dribbledrip!

(*Sensation. The* Gaffer *comes forward—now the perfect old family retainer*)

Gaffer. You rang, sir?
Sir Mortimer. Begad! Young Tom! I suppose you *are* Young Tom?
Gaffer. That's right, sir.
Sir Mortimer. Thought so. Never forget a face. Now tell me, Tom, how'd you like to be me batman? Eh? Ten pounds a year and all found. That suit you?
Gaffer. Suits me grand.
Sir Mortimer. Then consider yourself engaged.
Mrs Durden. Oh, Morty, I'm so glad.
Sir Mortimer. Then off we go to Mortiboy Hall.
Mrs Durden. They'll never look after you as well as I could. Why not stay at *The Flying Horse*—just till you've settled down?
Sir Mortimer. Begad, so I will! Look alive, Tom! Luggage, me boy, luggage!

(Gaffer *takes the luggage into "The Flying Horse", leaving the Hen*)

Blenkinsop (*coming forward with his microphone*) And now, Sir Mortimer, would you care to say a few words to the viewers?
Sir Mortimer. Begad, yes! Give me the speaking-tube. (*He blows into the microphone*) I've only just arrived in the Old Country but I've already noticed considerable changes. Some for the better——

(*He waves to the Village Girls.* Mrs Durden *steps between*)

—and others—well, the less said about them the better.

BLENKINSOP. I believe, sir, you've spent the last fifty years in Fairyland?
SIR MORTIMER. Yes.
BLENKINSOP. And what do you think of the internal situation?
SIR MORTIMER. Ah! Now that's just it. So long as the internal situation remains internal, then what with the balance of power on the one hand and the balance of payments on the other, why then, sir, the tide will turn in favour of those who are only waiting for the swing of the pendulum. And mark my words, sir, if those in the saddle fail to grasp the nettle instead of resting on their laurels, then the ship will founder with all hands. I think that takes care of the internal situation. Turning to the external situation . . .
BLENKINSOP (*hastily interposing*) And now, sir, would you like to tell us what you think of modern youth?
SIR MORTIMER (*slapping Jack on the shoulder*) I say there's nothing wrong with a generation that produces fine young fellers like Jack Durden—hero and leader of the great Beanstalk Expedition!

(*Cheers*)

MRS DURDEN (*embracing Jack*) My boy! A hero after all!
GRIMSHANK. Alice, come home! All is forgiven.
JACK. Oh no, Alderman. Alice is coming home with me.
GRIMSHANK. Now look 'ere . . .
JACK. Shake hands with your future son-in-law. Alice and I are going to be married at once by special licence.
SIR MORTIMER. Bless you, me children! Tell you what, we'll hold the reception at Mortiboy Hall.
MRS DURDEN. Out of the question. It's been taken over by the Ministry of Interference.
SIR MORTIMER. Begad!
MRS DURDEN. I know! We'll turn out the visitors and invite everybody to *The Flying Horse*.
SIR MORTIMER. A capital idea!
MRS DURDEN. And while we're about it, why not make it a double wedding? What do you say, Morty?
SIR MORTIMER. You take the words out of me mouth.
MRS DURDEN. Hear that, everybody? You're all invited——

(*The* CHILDREN *cheer*)

—and all drinks will be on the house.

(*Cheers from* GRIMSHANK, GAFFER *and* SIMON)

Run along, children, and tell your friends.

(*The* CHILDREN *exit, cheering*)

SIR MORTIMER. And now let's hold a Four Power Conference in the four-ale bar.

(GAFFER, SIMON, GRIMSHANK and ALICE *go into "The Flying Horse". The others are about to follow when* SIR MORTIMER *remembers the Magic Hen*)

Wait—surprise! (*He fetches the Hen*) Here's me present to the bride. Molly—Henrietta. Henrietta—Molly. (*He gives the Hen to Mrs Durden*)

MRS DURDEN. What a dear little hen! Is she a good layer?
SIR MORTIMER. Guaranteed to lay an egg every morning.
MRS DURDEN. Lovely! There's nothing I enjoy more than a nice new-laid egg.
JACK. But, Mother, you don't understand. Henrietta's a fairy hen. And she lays golden eggs—look!
MRS DURDEN. What a disappointment! I'd much rather have a real egg.
JACK. But Henrietta's eggs are hall-marked.

(ALICE *and* SIMON *appear at the door and window offering foaming tankards to* JACK *and* SIR MORTIMER, *who hurry inside leaving* MRS DURDEN *to confide in the Audience*)

MRS DURDEN. That's no proof that they're fresh. I ask you, what's the use of a golden egg when you want an egg for tea?

No. 14   SONG: "WHAT'S THE USE OF A GOLDEN EGG?" (MRS DURDEN)

  Of this absurd yet clever bird
   I often have been told;
  Her eggs new-laid are wholly made
   Of nineteen-carat gold,
  Which is amazing, I agree,
  But will you please explain to me—
  Oh,
  What's the use of a golden egg
  When you want an egg for tea?
  It can't be boiled and it can't be fried,
  It hasn't got a pretty little chick inside—
   Oh, Mr Philip Harben,
   Please tell us on TV
  What you can do with a golden egg
  When you want an egg for tea.

  This Golden Leghorn lays an egg
   Of solid gold each day—
  A special breed that's guaranteed
   To make your poultry pay;
  But golden eggs are hard to beat,
  And even harder still to eat,
  So,
  What's the use, etc.

Act III STORY OF JACK AND THE BEANSTALK 57

(*The Chorus is repeated with the Audience.*
Mrs Durden *exits into "The Flying Horse".*
Blenkinsop *enters* L *with his microphone and four scripts.*
Gaffer, Simon *and* Grimshank *come out of "The Flying Horse"*)

Blenkinsop. Now, where's my cast for *Country Magazine?* Oh, there you are! Come along, please, and take your scripts—we'll be on the air in two minutes.

(*They gloomily study the scripts*)

Gaffer. Can't make 'ead or tail o' this 'ere.
Blenkinsop. Idiot, you've got it upside down. Now, everybody, do please remember that the object of this type of programme is to create a definite illusion of unscripted spontaneity.
Gaffer. Wot's 'e say?
Grimshank. 'E means, let it rip!
Simon. An' no la-di-dah.
Gaffer. La-di-dah—'issen.
Blenkinsop. Quiet please! Listen, there's the signature tune.

(*Music—"The Painful Plough"*)

Don't rustle your scripts. Don't turn over two pages! And for heaven's sake be natural.

(*The music ends*)

Blenkinsop (*in a thick bucolic voice*) Well, listeners, this edition of *Country Magazine* is coming to you from the dear old village of Mangel-Wurzel-on-the-Wold. It's a sleepy old place is Mangel-Wurzel . . .

(*Pause.* Blenkinsop *glares at Grimshank.* Simon *nudges* Grimshank, *who begins to read painfully*)

Grimshank (*reading from his script*) "So that is wot you think is it Bill wait a minute Bob . . ."
Blenkinsop (*putting his hand over the microphone*) Stop! You're reading my line. I'm Bill—you're Bob.
Grimshank. Alderman Grimshank to you, me lad.
Blenkinsop. But we always use Christian names on the BBC. I assure you it doesn't mean a thing. Quick, cut to Speech Seventeen—that's you, Simon.
Simon (*reading*) "Aye, them were the days! Me an' my old woman reared fourteen children on nine bob a week, and allus a partridge in the pot come Sunday . . ."
Gaffer (*indignant*) You nivver reared no fourteen children! Not on no nine bob a week neether! I'm the only chap 'ere wot 'ad . . .
Blenkinsop. Line Seventeen, idiot—not Page Seventeen! Here,

cut the dialogue and come to the folk-song, Page Twenty-Two. (*Into the microphone, in an announcer's voice*) We must apologize to listeners for a short break in transmission. We now take you back to Mangel-Wurzel. (*In a bucolic voice*) And this is a place where they still cherish the old folk-songs. Come to *The Flying Horse* any Sunday lunch-time, and you'll hear this grand old tune as soon as they've finished the one o'clock news.

No. 15 TRIO (GRIMSHANK, SIMON *and* GAFFER)

GRIMSHANK. Come all ye country lads, and leave
  Your bebop and your swing;
Put on your ties of folky weave
  And let your voices ring;
For what can beat a country chap
  In a true-bred country tune
Before the nation takes its nap
  Of a Sunday afternoon?

ALL. Singing rumble bumpety bumpkin, O!
  And the smell of new-mown hay;
Singing dumble dumpety dumpkin, O!
  Down Mangel-Wurzel way:

GAFFER. The words may seem as daft to you
  As they seems daft to we,
But they earns an easy bob or two
  Upon the BBC.

SIMON. Sing hey for crusty Walter an'
  Sing hey for young Christine;
Sing hey for jolly old Farmer Dan—
  You all know who we mean:
The townsman in his easy chair
  Delights to plough and sow,
And take a breath of country air
  On the rural radio.

ALL. Singing rumble bumpety bumpkin, O!
  With a cock-a-lorum lay;
Singing dumble dumpety dumpkin, O!
  In a truly rural way:

GAFFER. We 'ad to use our pencil blue
  To keep the party clean,
For Grandad's verses wouldn't do
  In *Country Magazine*.
No, Grandad's verses wouldn't do
  In *Country Magazine!*

(ALL *exit.*
The BEANSTALK FAIRY *enters*)

Act III   STORY OF JACK AND THE BEANSTALK   59

BEANSTALK FAIRY.
>Now our story's nearly told—
>Mangel-Wurzel-on-the-Wold
>Still is doing very well;
>Full each café and hotel:
>Though upon the village green
>Beanstalk is no longer seen,
>Still the villagers can show
>Where the Beanstalk used to grow:
>Still the visitor may stand
>On the fringe of Fairyland;
>Still his mantelpiece may cheer
>With a Beanstalk souvenir—
>Ashtray, clock, or table-lighter
>Showing Jack, that doughty fighter,
>Facing fearful avalanches
>On the plastic Beanstalk branches.
>
>Fast the hours do fleet away
>Bringing happy nuptial-day:
>Hear the wedding-bells a-ringing!
>Hear the village children singing!

(*Wedding bells ring out.*
The BEANSTALK FAIRY *exits.*
The CHILDREN *enter, singing*)

No. 15a   CHORUS: *Repeat of No. 12* (CHILDREN)
>Come, lasses and lads,
>Get leave of your dads,
>To the wedding haste away,
>A lovely bride,
>Her groom beside,
>Has promised to obey,
>For Alice has got her Jack,
>And Molly is full of joy,
>For now she's Lady Morty, Morty,
>Morty, Mortiboy;
>For now she's Lady Morty, Morty,
>Morty, Mortiboy.

(*The* CHILDREN *do a country dance*)

No. 16   FINALE (FULL COMPANY)
(GRIMSHANK, GAFFER *and* SIMON *enter*)
CHORUS and TRIO: *Repeat of No. 15*

ALL.   With a rumble, bumpety bumpkin O,
>And a hip, hip, hip hooray!

	With a hey ding-dong and a wedding song
	Down Mangel-Wurzel way;
TRIO.	We'll drink the happy couple's health
	From morn till afternoon,
	And we'll still drink on when they have gone
	Upon their honeymoon.

(BLENKINSOP *and* MRS CROAKER *enter*)

CHORUS and DUET: *Repeat of No. 15*

BLENKINSOP.	With a dumble, dumpety dumpkin O,
	And the boys of the BBC
	With a shady shady lady O!
	A Wicked Fairy she:
MRS CROAKER.	O I have baked a wedding-cake—
	It's full of stones and glue,
	Of beetles dried and cyanide—
	I'll save a piece for you.

(MAISIE *enters, decorated. She trots round the stage*)

CHORUS: *Repeat of No. 5a*

ALL.	Hello, Maisie!
	Crazy Maisie!
	Hello, Maisie,
	You're quite a bridesmaid now.
	She shall have the finest hay,
	Finest hay,
	Finest hay,
	She shall have the finest hay,
	O, what a clever cow!

(*The* BEANSTALK FAIRY *enters*)

SOLO and CHORUS: *Repeat of No. 7*

BEENSTALK FAIRY.	Eeny, meeny, beany O!
	If you would make the Beanstalk grow
	This is the way,
	Together say,
	Eeny, meeny, beany O!
ALL.	Eeny, meeny, beany O! etc.

(*Wedding bells ring out*)

BRIDAL CHORUS

ALL.	Happy the bride,
	Happy the bride,

Happy the bride that the sun shines upon!
Happy the bride, etc.

(Sir Mortimer *and* Lady Mortiboy—*late* Mrs Durden—*enter*)

SOLO and CHORUS: *Repeat of No. 10*

SIR MORTIMER.
You can always trust the tenants of the family estate;
They're splendid chaps who touch their caps and think
   the Squire's great:
Begad, I'll soon be greater still—the Government has sent
To say I'm being scheduled as an Ancient Monument!

ALL.
You can always, etc.

(*Wedding bells ring out*)

BRIDAL CHORUS

ALL. Happy the bride, etc.

(JACK *and* ALICE *enter to cheers. They come down* C)

JACK. I didn't mean to make a speech today,
But still, there's just one thing I'd like to say—
We made the record-breaking Beanstalk climb
To give our friends a happy Christmas-time:
If you enjoyed the trip as much as we did
Our expedition certainly succeeded.

(*Cheers. They all come down*)

ENSEMBLE: *Repeat of No. 3*

DURDEN. Now everybody comes to Mangel-Wurzel,
To merry Mangel-Wurzel-on-the-Wold—

BEANSTALK FAIRY.
Though the Beanstalk may have gone
Still the legend lingers on—

GRIMSHANK. And the tourists flock like sheep into the fold,

JACK. The Edinburgh Festival has had it!

GAFFER. A million picture postcards we 'ave sold—

MRS DURDEN. And my son's the clever chap
Who has put upon the map
Enchanted Mangel-Wurzel-on-the-Wold.

ALL. Yes, our Jack's the clever chap, etc.

(*During the final Number the Hen is passed to* SIR MORTIMER)

SOLO: *Repeat of No. 14*

JACK.
Now is the time to say good-bye
To our comrades old and new;
If you've enjoyed our Christmas play
Come to Mangel-Wurzel for your holiday,
And we'll ask Henrietta,
To see what she can do—
Perhaps she'll lay while you're down our way,
A golden egg for you!

(SIR MORTIMER *produces a golden egg*)

FINAL CHORUS: *Repeat of No. 14*

ALL. Now is the time, etc.

CURTAIN

FURNITURE AND PROPERTY PLOT

ACT I

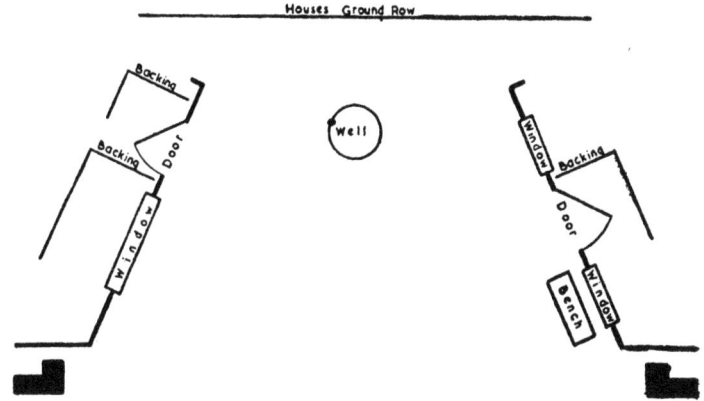

On stage: Beanstalk in well
Broom (SIMON)
Decorated mug (GAFFER)

Off stage: Pail (JACK)
Jug (MRS DURDEN)
Handbell and town-crier's hat (GAFFER)
Carving-knife (GRIMSHANK)
Red curtain on curtain-rod (GRIMSHANK)
Rose, fan and mantilla (MRS DURDEN)
Lamp (ALICE)
Toy watering-cans (FAIRIES)
Haversack (ALICE)
Telescope (GAFFER)

Personal: Handkerchief (MRS DURDEN)
Purse. *In it:* beans (BEANSTALK FAIRY)

ACT II

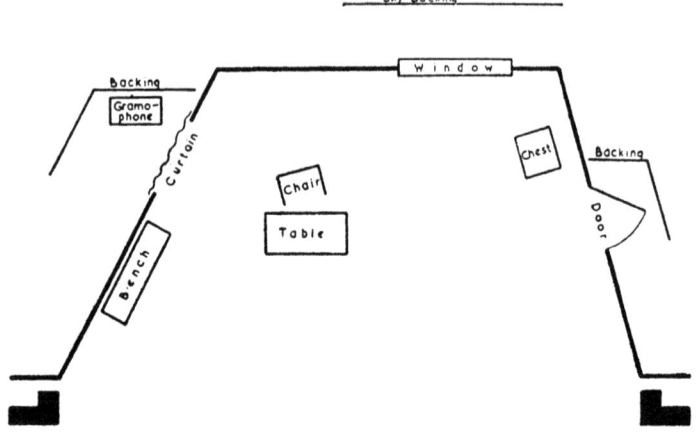

On stage: Bench
Chest. *On it:* Magic Hen. *In it:* golden egg
Jar of Mandragora's Drowsy Syrup
"Private" notice on curtain
Lecturer's pointer
In recess behind curtain:
    Horn gramophone and records
    Union Jack
    Pith helmet
    Toy gun
    Water pistol
    Toy telescope
    Top hat
    Fancy waistcoat
    Gloves
    Cane
    Dispatch-case
    Flower for buttonhole
    Handkerchief
    Shoe-brush
    Clothes-brush

Off stage: Tea-tray. *On it:* newspaper, teapot, cup and saucer, etc.
    (CROAKER)
Beanstalk
Gladstone bag (CROAKER)
Umbrella (CROAKER)

STORY OF JACK AND THE BEANSTALK 65

    Shopping-bag (MRS CROAKER)
    Blunderbuss (CROAKER)
    Wands (FAIRIES)

Personal: Ribbons (FAIRIES)
    Monocle (SIR MORTIMER)
    Dispatch (SIR MORTIMER)
    Whistle (1ST FAIRY)
    Crown (BEANSTALK FAIRY)
    Order of Titania (BEANSTALK FAIRY)

ACT III

On stage: On cottages: TV aerials and signs, etc. (see stage direction)
    In "*The Flying Horse*" *window:* Sign—"House Full"
    In shop window: Sign—"Salmon Teas"
    Beanstalk (grown) with ribbons attached

Off stage: 2 beer-mugs (SIMON)
    Microphone (BLENKINSOP)
    Cine-camera (BLENKINSOP)
    Parachute (SIR MORTIMER)
    Sir Mortimer's top-hat
    The Croakers' bags (SIR MORTIMER)
    Magic Hen (SIR MORTIMER)
    2 beer-mugs (SIMON and ALICE)
    4 scripts (BLENKINSOP)

Personal: Peaked cap and ticket-punch (GAFFER)
    Golden egg (SIR MORTIMER)

LIGHTING PLOT

ACT I

Property fittings required: lamp
    Exterior. Daylight
    The MAIN ACTING AREA covers the whole stage

To open: daylight

Cue 1	MAISIE *chases* MRS DURDEN *off stage* Dim lights to moonlight, and bring up lights in lower windows	(page 18)
Cue 2	ALICE *appears with a lamp* Bring up lights slightly up R	(page 20)
Cue 3	*The* FAIRIES *dance off* Take out lights in windows. Bring up lighting to daylight, at dawn	(page 22)

ACT II

Property fittings required: none
    Interior. Early morning
    The MAIN ACTING AREAS are up R by the recess, C by the table, L by the chest, and up LC by the window
    The APPARENT SOURCE OF LIGHT is the window up LC

To open: daylight

No cues

ACT III

Property fittings required: none
    Exterior. Daylight
    The MAIN ACTING AREA covers the whole stage

To open: early summer morning

No cues

MADE AND PRINTED IN GREAT BRITAIN BY
LATIMER TREND & COMPANY LTD PLYMOUTH

MADE IN ENGLAND